Non-Fungible Tokens (NFTs)

Andrea Sestino • Gianluigi Guido
Alessandro M. Peluso

Non-Fungible Tokens (NFTs)

Examining the Impact on Consumers
and Marketing Strategies

Andrea Sestino
Ionian Department of Law,
Economics, Environment
University of Bari Aldo Moro
Taranto, Italy

Gianluigi Guido
Department of Management and
Economics
University of Salento
Lecce, Italy

Alessandro M. Peluso
Department of Management and
Economics
University of Salento
Lecce, Italy

ISBN 978-3-031-07202-4   ISBN 978-3-031-07203-1   (eBook)
https://doi.org/10.1007/978-3-031-07203-1

This Palgrave Macmillan imprint is published by the registered company Springer Nature Switzerland AG.
The registered company address is: Gewerbestrasse 11, 6330 Cham, Switzerland

FOREWORD

Non-Fungible Tokens (NFTs) have caught the attention of the public, investors, and collectors in a big way through the publicity surrounding sales in the tens of millions of dollars. Digital artists benefit by eliminating galleries and dealers, as well as in potentially earning royalties on future sales of their NFTs. It is an exciting and confusing time for several reasons. Markets for the sale and resale of NFTs have developed and prices are being tracked and forecasted. Because the sale of the NFT does not normally include IP (intellectual property rights), you can own the NFT for a piece of digital art without having the right to print it on a t-shirt. You can own an NFT clip of a LeBron James basketball play without the right to put the clip on your blog or website. And you can own an NFT of a performance by the latest K-pop boy band without the right to sell the performance to someone else—the NFT yes, the music no.

Confusing? This book is for you.

There is something brand new here and many questions are answered while with others we can only guess. Will the NFT bubble burst? Could future technologies make it possible to store not only the meta-data of NFTs on an Ethereum blockchain but the underlying physical asset as well? And now that books, messages, music, movies, and more have become digital, are available through streaming access without ownership, and are thus far dependent on the continued existence of a game, virtual world, or other platform, will NFTs and the blockchain give us inalienable access and cross-platform interoperability? Will the land that we have developed in Decentraland and the avatar that we have created in Fortnite be accessible in Somnium? Will there be enough people in the Metaverse that I can wear my 3D digital outfit in public without revealing that the emperor has no [real] clothes?

Stay tuned.

Meanwhile get acquainted with the basics in this book. It also traces the effects of materialism and status consciousness on buying and owning non-material and largely invisible NFT assets—with some surprising results.

Look forward to this timely and well-conceived book!

Schulich School of Business   Russell Belk
York University
Toronto, ON, Canada

ACKNOWLEDGMENTS

The authors would like to thank Prof. Giovanni Pino, at University of Chieti–Pescara, for his contribution to an early version of Chap. 2 and Prof. Cesare Amatulli, at University of Bari, for sharing his views on fashion and luxury markets.

A sincere appreciation for their kind support goes also to Ms. Cindy Pedone, for digitally illustrating the stimuli used in the questionnaires; to Mr. Shawn White, at Fallen Apple, for his editorial work on the text; and, last but not least, to Ms. Liz Barlow, at Palgrave, for her constant assistance and patience.

CONTENTS

About the Authors

Andrea Sestino is, currently, Ph.D. candidate in Management and Marketing at University of Bari "Aldo Moro," under the supervision of the second author. He is expert collaborator for the Cabinet of the Italian Minister of Economic Development, in fields related to artificial intelligence, internet-of-things applications, and business digitalization. He holds an M.Sc. in Business Management at Sapienza University, Rome, Italy, and has been R&D specialist in the field of applied industrial research for business digital transition in several private and public research projects. He has published in international peer-reviewed journals, such as *Technovation, Technology Analysis & Strategic Management, Journal of Learning and Intellectual Capital, Journal of Financial Service Marketing, International Journal of Cultural Heritage & Sustainable Development, International Journal of Healthcare and Pharmaceutical Marketing, British Food Journal, Current Research in Environmental Sustainability, Journal of Sport & Tourism, International Journal of Electronic Trade, Italian Journal of Marketing, Italian Journal of Management, SN Business & Economics, Psychological Reports, International Journal of Marketing Studies, Technology in Society.*

Gianluigi Guido (Ph.D. in Management Sciences, University of Cambridge, UK) is Full Professor of Marketing at the Department of Management and Economics of the University of Salento, Italy, where he is director of the Ph.D. Program in Digital Transformation and Sustainability. He has been professor at the LUISS University of Rome, at the Faculty of Psychology of the University of Rome "Sapienza," and at the Faculty of Statistics of the University of Padua, Italy. He has also been a visiting researcher at the Department of Marketing of the University of Florida, Gainesville; and visiting scholar at the Department of Psychology of the Stanford University. He was director of the Social Sciences Department of the ISUFI (Istituto Superiore Universitario per la Formazione Interdisciplinare) at the University of Salento.He has been lecturer in 150 national and international conferences and has published more than 300 scientific publications and articles in international academic journals, including *Cambridge Research Papers, European Journal of Marketing, International Journal of Advertising, International Journal of Research in Marketing, Italian Journal of Marketing, Journal of Advertising Research, Journal of Brand Management, Journal of Business Ethics, Journal of Business & Industrial Marketing, Journal of Business Research, Journal of Consumer Research, Journal of Economic Psychology, Journal of Marketing Management, Journal of Product & Brand Management, Journal of Retailing and Consumer Services, Journal of Services Marketing, Long Range Planning, Marketing Letters, Psychology & Marketing, Recherche et Applications en Marketing, Research Policy, SN Business & Economics, Technovation*, and others. With Palgrave Macmillan, he has published *Sustainable Luxury Brands: Evidence from Research and Implications for Managers*, Palgrave Advances in Luxury Series, 2017 (co-authors C. Amatulli, M. De Angelis, and M. Costabile), with an introduction by Richard Bagozzi and Philip Kotler.

Alessandro M. Peluso (Ph.D. in Economic and Quantitative Methods for Market Analysis) is Associate Professor of Business Management at the Department of Management and Economics of the University of Salento, Italy, where he teaches Business Management and Destination Marketing. Prof. Peluso has been contract professor at the LUISS University and LUISS Business School, Rome, where he has been lectured in advertising, marketing, marketing strategies, visual marketing, social marketing, and marketing research.His research interests are in the field of consumer behavior with a special focus on the psychological drivers of sustainable consumption, social communication effectiveness, and the social transmission of information via word of mouth. His scientific production comprises more than 100 publications, including three research monographs, 70 articles in international refereed journals—including *Computers in Human Behavior, European Journal of Marketing, Human Resource Management Journal, International Journal of Research in Marketing,*

Journal of Advertising Research, Journal of Brand Management, Journal of Business Ethics, Journal of Business Research, Journal of Consumer Marketing, Journal of Consumer Research, Journal of Marketing Research, Journal of Product and Brand Management, Journal of Retailing and Consumer Services, Psychology and Marketing, Research Policy, Tourism Management, Trends in Food Science and Technology—together with several book chapters and conference proceedings.

LIST OF FIGURES

LIST OF TABLES

CHAPTER 1

Introduction

Abstract This chapter explains how recent phenomena, such as the pandemic and the diffusion of teleworking, have speeded up the adoption of quite a few technological innovations. Among these, the so-called *Non-Fungible Tokens (NFTs)*—that is, the cryptographic ownership certificates of digital objects (e.g., artworks, music plays, fashion products)—have the capacity to revolutionize the e-commerce as we know it. NFTs might reshape consumers' relationships with products and, in turn, with their own *extended-selves*, by changing their ideas of possession in an increasingly dematerialized world.

Keywords Non-Fungible Tokens (NFTs) • Technological innovations • Digitization • Possession • Consumer extended-self

In the last two years, the COVID-19 pandemic has forced many individuals to work and socialize remotely by using various communication platforms (e.g., Teams, Zoom, Meet, and so on). Through these platforms, people usually connect from home, from their room, in conditions in which they often find themselves after a long stay without interacting with strangers.

If, in the past, the social representation of oneself could count on the fact that, leaving one's apartments, one was physically prepared to meet people by presenting himself adequately to social appointments (for example, in a tie for work, or in evening clothes for a gala dinner), today to meet people on these platforms, habits have often encouraged laziness and, with it, less respectful behaviors of social custom. It is not an extraordinary fact, although bordering on ridicule, that very often to attend a business meeting or university lecture held online, the manager or the professor on duty wears everything from the waist up, reserving a more "leisure" outfit for the part that is not framed by the camera (depending on the season, sweatpants, shorts, or even underwear!). Moreover, when connecting from home, the alternative offered by these IT platforms at the time in which we write these lines is to frame in the background of the speaker either the room in which you are actually—with all the possible disorder that could be in your home (in the past, normally hidden from most and known only to close family members)—or some anonymous backgrounds to choose from, such as an empty room, the New York skyline, a Hawaiian countryside, or the logo of your company (as for maximum customization).

Is it likely to believe that all of this will remain unchanged over time? We do not think that, with the increasing spread of teleworking, distance learning, and the development of many other teleconferencing activities (weddings, anniversaries, birthdays, and so on)—either, unfortunately, encouraged by pandemic crises or, positively, by the possibilities offered by telematics connections to save on the costs of transport, physical transfer, logistics, or leasing—the interactions that take place on these communication platforms will remain the same as today. We do not think it is possible.

The development of technology has accustomed us to epochal changes in a short time: The recent birth of the so-called Metaverse, that is, a virtual and parallel reality in which each of us—as well as the objects that we possess and of which we surround ourselves—can be represented differently, is leading us toward horizons not yet fully imagined, certainly destined to change quickly and radically with the development of technology. It would seem that each of us will not be able to escape from this alternative universe over time, whether one is a digital native, apparently accustomed to such changes or an older person who often "undergoes" these innovations or even opposes them (Guido, 2014). It is not possible today to imagine with certainty how these innovations will assert themselves or induce changes—perhaps, even exceptional ones—in the future. However, we can analyze some phenomena that, also now, can generate changes in the way people relate to others and, above all, adapt their consumption behaviors in relation to others and to themselves facing such innovations.

1 THE PHENOMENON OF NON-FUNGIBLE TOKENS (NFTs)

The phenomenon of the so-called Non-Fungible Tokens—or NFTs—regards a recent technological innovation that could greatly alter the way people buy, possess, use or—in a word—consume goods in their lives. NFTs are cryptographic ownership certificates that represent intangible assets, such as an image, an online feature, or a digital object that are not interchangeable. Such assets gain their authenticity by belonging to a digital register based on the "Blockchain" technology, which is able to securely list records and linked them together using cryptography. As this registry is shared among several computers, it is possible to guarantee the originality and immutability of the related information over time. Unlike other tokens (such as cryptocurrencies), as the name indicates, NFTs are non-fungible—that is, non-replaceable objects. They are totally unique pieces, at least in a digital sense. Those who own them can claim an easily verifiable property right through the visibility of such information on the blockchain network.

Let's imagine how the above-mentioned scenario set out for example could change with the development and diffusion of NFTs through the blockchain technology. In the near future (perhaps, even by the time this book is published), some people connecting to an online meeting via an IT platform (Teams, Zoom, Meet, and so on) could have their video background be a virtual environment, furnished through the purchase and display (if not exhibition) of authentic NFTs. They could display an NFT painting behind themselves, purchased from the "OpenSea" digital art site or maybe from an auction house. Such sales are already underway: It is well-known the case of the digital artist named Beeple, who recently sold an NFT collage entitled "Everyday" for over 60 million dollars; even more recently, another artist named Pak sold an NFT entitled "The Merge" to almost 30,000 collectors pitching together for a total cost of 91.8 million dollars. As a matter of fact, it is not strange nowadays to find NFT artworks already populating art galleries and museums all over the world.

Similarly, communication platforms may eventually allow users to access an NFT-based digital wardrobe, where their on-screen clothing is adjusted to fit the occasion (similar to how some photo filters add silly glasses to one's face). Thus, even if users are wearing comfortable clothes or joining IT platforms from a cluttered room, they can appear properly dressed in a tastefully decorated virtual environment, all done through the purchase of

NFTs. Through a combination of photographic filters and NFT products (e.g., digital furniture, backgrounds, and so on), we might achieve enhanced versions of ourselves—more elegant, better fitted, wrinkle-free—until the time when technology allows us to participate through digital alter egos—that is, *avatars*, or digital representations of ourselves (Yee & Bailenson, 2007)—that are immune to deterioration.

The reality of such situations is already upon us. The expansion of the mixing of real and virtual environments in the Metaverse is the case-in-point. Well-known clothing brands (i.e., Dolce & Gabbana, Gucci, RTFKT Studios) are experimenting with selling high fashion clothes and shoes in the virtual space reserved for avatars. The prices of those items parallel their counterparts (i.e., the comparatively high physical goods), because they usually satisfy the same underlying desire to flaunt users' ability to afford luxurious garments. In the virtual Metaverse, the opportunities to consume are doubled with respect to the physical environment, but also problems. An Indian couple, who recently married, invited the bulk of their guests virtually, in response to COVID restrictions. The guests attended the function through their avatars and they could have the wedding lunch directly delivered to their homes. Whereas, in another (distressing) example, a British woman, who was participating to a video game (i.e., a beta-test for Facebook's virtual reality app Horizon Worlds), alleged that she was verbally and sexually assaulted by male avatars within minutes of joining the game. In response, the company had to establish a 4-foot (i.e., 1 meter and 20 centimeters) "personal space" boundary between players' avatars since then!

2   NFTs and the Consumer's Extended Self

If to live means to consume, it is therefore fair to ask ourselves: How will this shift in consumption change the way that we live? In particular, how much can the development of NFTs' technology contribute to modifying consumers' relationship with products and services, especially as technology strips away the former's materiality? How will NFTs influence consumers' degree of materialism (when the owned products are increasingly dematerialized), their degree of novelty acceptance (especially for non-digital natives who struggle with continuous technological changes), or their relationship with goods and, by extension, other consumers (such as displaying conspicuous purchases and having them be understood)? To borrow from Hirsch's (1976) seminal book on positional goods: How will consumers be able to realize the social utility of their purchases?

In this regard, Russell Belk (1988, 2013)—a leading authority on consumption, consumer culture, and consumer behavior—has provided a useful framework for understanding the major changes that digitization imposes on asset possession. According to Belk, consumers' effort to project a sense of self into a digital environment can be broken down into five elements: dematerialization, sharing, re-embodiment, co-construction of self, and distributed memory. This framework offers a foundation for understanding consumers' purchase of products via NFTs, and more broadly, the appeal of "hybrid goods" that merge the physical and the digital.

If we consider the *dematerialization* introduced by digitization, then NFTs are neither products nor services, but a hybrid species. Like services, NFTs are immaterial: They do not confer the possession of a physical asset but rather a claimable property right. This would include digitally reproducible artworks (e.g., a photo, a video, an online file), or the right to use a certain digital key that allows access to some virtual platform (e.g., a video game, an exclusive community, an account). Unlike services, however, NFTs do not require the owner's direct participation, a large skilled workforce, or even a specific physical location to be consumed. Unlike products, one cannot easily flaunt NFTs in the same way as a sports car or jewelry, especially outside of virtual environments. So, one could believe that NFTs mainly satisfy consumers' "internalized goals" (Amatulli & Guido, 2011, 2012), as collectors do just for the sake of their ownership. In such cases, individuals are mainly motivated by their desire to experience intimate feelings and emotions. Those who buy NFTs would do so for overriding reasons of self-gratification, hedonism, pursuit of originality, belonging to an elite group or to a culture. Consequently, NFTs primarily align with the idea of inconspicuous consumption, which entails a dissociation from displaying possessions and wealth (Wu et al., 2017) and the use of subtle signals of status whose meaning can only be decoded by people with the appropriate knowledge (Berger & Ward, 2010). It is important to note that dematerialization does not exclude attachment; indeed, the drive to own these digital products can be fetishistic. Yet, the singularization of such virtual possessions is almost—although not quite—the same, compared to that which occurs in the real world (Belk, 2013).

At first glance, it would seem that the dematerialization enabled by NFTs allows for a more democratic distribution of wealth, as they contain the possibility of *sharing* the same objects—for example, products or art-works—among multiple users. Consider the case of Julian Lennon, who recently auctioned the NFTs of objects belonging to his father John, including guitars, clothes, and even the manuscript of "Hey Jude" (The Beatles' song dedicated to him). The ability to sell them in the form of NFTs allowed the bidder to avoid materially depriving himself of the memorabilia, while still earning good money by giving buyers exclusive access to these special items. On the one hand, such an option might be an effective, albeit paid, way to enable the sharing of unique artifacts that would otherwise remain under lock and key. On the other hand, especially to a traditional consumer accustomed to transactions on real markets, the same thing could appear as a fraud, considering that there would be nothing physical for a fan to show emotional or fetish attachment to (e.g., an autograph or a real object belonging to the celebrity). In the "Age of mechanical reproduction," to quote the title of a famous essay by Walter Benjamin (1936/1969), it would be clearly seen that a real autograph costs many times more than a photocopy of it, as it allows fans—some-how—to "possess" an original piece of their idol, be part of his aura, of his world. In this sense, while NFTs seem to create the opportunity for more people to share in the possession of exclusive goods, frustrations may erupt over the fact that, in reality, only a few people have actual physical possession of the linked object (see the "Joyless economy" of Tibor Scitovsky, 1976). There could be a recovery of credibility for those assets that, from the outset, are virtual, the exclusive possession of which could also make sense in the real economy. Consider, for example, how many of today's literary masterpieces are produced on a computer via word processing software. If all the early versions of a book that went to print and became a best seller were sold via NFTs, that would represent a real investment in something irreproducible and exclusive. During his life, the Welsh poet Dylan Thomas used to sell, in order to survive, the original sheets on which he had written his poems; today, an author could sell the original files of his books written on the computer for a fee.

The possession of NFTs also enables *re-embodiment*, that is, the ability to modify one's avatar, thereby realizing one's strangest identity fantasies, or even multiple aspirational selves (Eladhari, 2007). In the real world, we all see ourselves a unique based on our age, environmental conditions, and social circumstances (Amatulli et al., 2018; Guido et al., 2016); it is also true that our self-image often differs from how most other people see us, due to an emphasis on external factors rather than internal changes. The virtual world offers an opportunity to align these two images through our avatars, that is, the digital representations of ourselves. Through our avatars, we can control many of our imperfections (e.g., obesity, old age, physical handicaps) and exhibit our idealized selves. In this context, NFTs represent a powerful marketing device, allowing people access to virtual products that can help them create their own characters in online environments (whether these be virtual games, blogs, web pages, or social networks). Such enhancement could range from the level of accessories to the entire body appearance. In this way, NFTs would allow us to transcend materialism and express our desired self to other people.

This situation also captures the idea of the *co-construction of the self*: As human beings, individuals need a reference community from which to draw support in terms of emotions, safety, and survival. In this sense, purchasing NFT-based products is a way to belong to communities that have the same interests and objectives. Take, for example, the new field of "generative art"—that is, artworks that are produced by algorithms capable of independently assembling different modules established by the artist or programmer. Despite comprising recurring elements, these productions are always unique. Because these collections encompass massive numbers of NFTs, buyers can acquire individual compositions that satisfy their taste at a modest cost, while also joining a larger community that enjoys such pieces and engages with the broader lifestyle. A clear case in point is the "Bored apes" collection, which Sotheby's has sold in lots for millions of dollars (Lee, 2021). Through social networking sites like Twitter, people can show off their NFTs as a signal of their belonging to a social circle, a sub-culture, or a lifestyle. The efforts required to represent oneself in this socially idealized form within online networks could be, especially for the youngest, digital natives, very high—namely, the price of a distortion in one's development on a psychological level, even with the rise of real compulsive and addictive pathologies.

Finally, the characteristics of NFTs lend themselves to commercializing individuals' *distributed memory*, although this point has not been adequately addressed in the current literature. One of the authors of this volume (Guido, 2002) predicted some of these objectives long before virtuality and the Internet—much less NFTs—were pervasive. Distributed memory reflects the desire to digitize—and, thereby, preserve—elements, or even the entirety, of one's life. Such a desire predates NFTs, and even the Internet, but the concept is becoming increasingly salient as technology becomes more accessible. At the beginning of the last century, people could have, at most, few photos or a portrait of themselves, whereas people today can already film nearly every day of their lives at little expense. In this context, NFTs could constitute a technical vehicle for not only documenting but also commercializing one's existence. NFTs represent an expansion of what is sellable. Online influencers do that in a general way, while NFTs could allow each of us the marketing of our most intimate sphere: our telephone book, our personal memory or, even, our friendships and private relationships. Microsoft engineer Gordon Bell (see Bell & Gemmell, 2009) was the first to attempt to digitize his entire life, scanning photos, documents, work notes, and anything else reproducible with the technology. An individual's digital archive—composed of pictures, records, books, souvenirs, letters, videos, and so on—would constitute a meaningful, albeit immaterial, autobiographical memory. Taken further, NFTs could virtually immortalize our virtual selves by providing a virtual "place," a gravesite, where at death we can bury ourselves without disappearing from the collective memory. A sort of eternal avatar of ourselves that survives us, where to stay "hibernated" in our virtual self—hopefully an ideal one, which adheres to our vision of ourselves—in the hope of being rediscovered and considered at least beyond our earthly existence.

REFERENCES

Amatulli, C., & Guido, G. (2011). Determinants of Purchasing Intention for Fashion Luxury Goods in the Italian Market: A Laddering Approach. *Journal of Fashion Marketing and Management, 15*(1), 123–136.

Amatulli, C., & Guido, G. (2012). Externalized vs. Internalized Consumption of Luxury Goods: Propositions and Implications for Luxury Retail Marketing. *The International Review of Retail, Distribution and Consumer Research, 22*(2), 189–207.

Amatulli, C., Peluso, A. M., Guido, G., & Yoon, C. (2018). When Feeling Younger Depends on Others: The Effects of Social Cues on Older Consumers. *Journal of Consumer Research, 45*(4), 691–709.

Belk, R. W. (1988). Possessions and the Extended Self. *Journal of Consumer Research, 15*(2), 139–168.

Belk, R. W. (2013). Extended Self in a Digital World. *Journal of Consumer Research, 40*(3), 477–500.

Bell, G., & Gemmell, J. (2009). The E-Memory Revolution. *Library Journal, 134*(15), 20–23.

Benjamin, W. (1936/1969). The Work of Art in the Age of Mechanical Reproduction. In H. Arendt (Ed.), *Illuminations* (pp. 214–218). Schocken Books.

Berger, J., & Ward, M. (2010). Subtle Signals of Inconspicuous Consumption. *Journal of Consumer Research, 37*(4), 555–569.

Eladhari, M. (2007). The Player's Journey. In J. P. Williams & J. H. Smith (Eds.), *The Players' Realm: Studies on the Culture of Video Games and Gaming* (pp. 171–187). Jefferson, NC.

Guido, G. (2002). Dalla Personalizzazione alla Virtualizzazione del Marketing dei Luoghi. In L. Biggiero & A. Sammarra (Eds.), *Apprendimento, Identità e Marketing del Territorio* (pp. 96–107). Carocci Editore.

Guido, G. (2014). *Il Comportamento di Consumo degli Anziani: Effetti per le Strategie di Marketing delle Imprese.* Il Mulino.

Guido, G., Prete, M. I., Pichierri, M., Pino, G., & Peluso, A. M. (2016). *Beyond Ethical Consumption: Religious-like Behaviours and Marketing Habits for Fervid Attachment to Brands.* Peter Lang.

Hirsch, F. (1976). *Social Limits to Growth.* Harvard University Press.

Lee, E. (2021). The Bored Ape Business Model: Decentralized Collaboration via Blockchain and NFTs. Retrieved November 30, 2021, from https://doi.org/10.2139/ssrn.3963881

Scitovsky, T. (1976). *The Joyless Economy: An Inquiry into Human Satisfaction and Consumer Dissatisfaction.* Oxford University Press.

Wu, T. Y., Tseng, Y. M., Huang, S. S., & Lai, Y. C. (2017). Non-Repudiable Provable Data Possession Scheme with Designated Verifier in Cloud Storage Systems. *IEEE Access, 5,* 19333–19341.

Yee, N., & Bailenson, J. (2007). The Proteus Effect: The effect of Transformed Self-representation on Behavior. *Human Communication Research, 33*(3), 271–290.

The Concept and Technicalities of NFTs

Abstract This chapter conceptualizes NFTs, describes their creation process, and illustrates their *main characteristics* (i.e., unicity, indivisibility, and scarcity), which differentiate them from Fungible Tokens (e.g., cryptocurrencies). It presents the technical aspects of NFTs and the main technology behind them, the so-called *Blockchain*, which essentially consists of a set of software applications that allow data storage in a transparent, decentralized, immutable ways.

Keywords NFTs' definition • Fungible Tokens (FTs) • Blockchain technology

1 Definition of Non-Fungible Tokens (NFTs) and Their Value

The business associated with NFTs exploded in the first half of 2021, capturing the attention of researchers and professionals (Wired, 2021). Simply put, NFTs are digital ownership certificates that are based on the so-called blockchain technology, whose possession proves the indisputable proprietorship of a purchased digital asset (Wang et al., 2021). In the first half of 2021, blockchain-based applications, such as NFTs and cryptocurrencies (which, on the contrary of NFTs, are fungible), generated a sales volume around 2.5 billion dollars (Forbes, 2021).

© The Author(s), under exclusive license to Springer Nature
Switzerland AG 2022
A. Sestino et al., *Non-Fungible Tokens (NFTs)*,
https://doi.org/10.1007/978-3-031-07203-1_2

To better clarify the utility of NFTs, we note that the term "token" should be intended as an item with a particular and symbolic value (Oliveira et al., 2018). In IT, a token is a set of digital information able to identify a specific purchasable object. More specifically, a token is a set of digital information within a blockchain that confers some rights to that particular object. Translated into the digital world, the token in an NFT represents a certificate that attests to the authenticity, uniqueness, and ownership of a digital object, such as an image, a music file, a video, an online game, or even a tweet or a post on major social media. In this sense, the NFT indisputably identifies the digital property of such an object (Singh & Singh, 2021).

As in the goods market, these items may be both fungible and non-fungible. Fungible Tokens (FTs), like fungible goods, are replaceable and measurable by nature (e.g., a kilogram of wheat, a liter of oil, an ounce of gold; Durham, 1965). Cryptocurrencies—such as Bitcoins—are the most famous example of FTs, as they can be traded or exchanged for one another. They are also equal in value—one dollar is always worth another dollar; one Bitcoin is always equal to another Bitcoin. Their fungibility makes them a trusted means of conducting transactions using the same blockchain technology which is behind NFTs. Differently from cryptocurrencies, NFTs as non-fungible goods cannot be replaced with others of the same type, as their characteristics are dissimilar or coincidental (e.g., as for houses, buildings, tailor-made services, artworks, musical tracks, and so on). Thus, regardless of whether the economic function of each unit is similar (e.g., as for houses, buildings, and similar ones) or diametrically different (e.g., as for artworks or musical tracks), each asset possesses different characteristics that imbue it with unique value.

Against this backdrop, one can begin to understand the potentialities of NFTs. For decades, digital items have been provided and proposed through *ad hoc* free online platforms, both legal (e.g., Google Images, YouTube) or illegal (e.g., as for the black market) ones (Wilson et al., 2021). In either case, the content is effortlessly replicated and its authenticity is difficult to prove (Chohan & Paschen, 2021). The original owners—for example, musicians, artists, brand holders—have struggled to verify and profit from their digital content (e.g., digital art or collectibles). In addition, consumers have found it difficult to purchase authentic digital content; until now, consumers could only "own" non-digital items such as branded clothing and printed content (Wilson et al., 2021). With NFTs, however, companies and entrepreneurs can monetize their content while giving consumers the assurance of their ownership. Two curious examples come from recent advertising moves: Taco Bell has sold NFTs of tacos pieces to confer consumers a sense of owning those pieces; Pizza Hut did the same with "limited edition" NFT-sets of pizza slices (Chohan & Paschen, 2021).

As these cases suggest, there is a growing interest in using NFTs to stimulate a new paradigm around business value propositions and intellectual work. The *momentum* is driven mainly by three factors: the opportunity for creators to exercise and transmit the rights associated with such items; the possibility for users to boast about owning such objects; and the facilitation of marketing and advertising strategies that can leverage such items' uniqueness, which we will discuss in greater detail in the following chapters.

1.1   The Origin of NFTs and Their Characteristics

The genesis of the spread of NFTs can be traced back to 2017, and it is linked to the funny phenomenon of "CryptoKitties." CryptoKitties were figurines of digital kittens in the form of NFTs, parts of a game created by the Canadian company Dapper Labs (Serada et al., 2021). All these figurines were one of a kind and exchangeable, just like collectibles. By leveraging on CryptoKitties experiences, many digital artists have begun to propose their contents under the NFT form in an attempt to create unreplaceable contents, infused by uniqueness. Such efforts have catalyzed great interest from users and the media and have concerned many creativity markets, such as art, fashion, and music (Wang et al., 2021).

As mentioned above, a digital artist, Mike Winkelmann, known as Beeple, sold an NFT consisting of a collage containing 5000 unique digital works in the form of images, taken over the course of 13 years, for almost 70 million dollars (Forbes, 2021). Taking a different tact, the contemporary artist known as Banksy literally burned one of his artworks in a live stream in order to confer unicity upon the digital copy that was then tokened. The piece was then sold in the digital marketplace at four times the price of the physical item. Some of the best-known of these NFTs' marketplaces are OpenSea, Rarible, and SuperRare. As of mid-2021, they have each recorded transaction volumes amounting to tens of millions of dollars (Focus, 2021).

There are substantial differences between FTs and NFTs traded on digital platforms. Whereas FTs are divisible into fractions, NFTs are not mutually interchangeable and thus totally indivisible (Wang et al., 2021). This contrasts with cryptocurrencies, as Bitcoin and other network or utility tokens which are inherently fungible (Dwyer, 2015). Thus, an NFT can be thought of as a certificate of ownership that uniquely, precisely, and indisputably identifies the possession of an object (Ante, 2021). Interestingly, by leveraging their unicity, NFTs may be used to simulate and create the concept of "scarcity," and specifically in terms of provable digital scarcity, digital ownership, and/or the possibility of interoperability of resources on multiple platforms (Chohan & Paschen, 2021).

To summarize the previous sections, an NFT is a special type of cryptographic token with a unique content. It is not mutually interchangeable and is, thus, rare by the nature of its unicity. NFTs can contain any kind of item or product that is digitally created or translated from real-world content (Evans, 2019; Wang et al., 2021). Moreover, NFTs represent an evolution of physical ownership because they allow someone to be the "true" owner of a unique digital asset (Nadini et al., 2021; Wang et al., 2021). Due to their peculiar characteristics, NFTs can be proposed, traded, sold, or transferred through digital platforms (see Table 2.1).

1.2   The NFTs' Creation Process

The creation of NFTs is enabled by numerous blockchain-based marketplace platforms, such as MetaMask, Bitski, and OpenSea (Forbes, 2021). When users upload a file, those platforms guarantee the "transformation" of an item into a blockchain-based object and certify its uniqueness. For

Table 2.1   The NFTs' characteristics

NFT characteristics	Meaning
Unicity	NFTs are unique and, thus, there are no identical copies of the same NFT in circulation. Indeed, each NFT has a specific digital identifier (ID), such that the pair "contract address-token ID" is unique within the reference ecosystem (i.e., the blockchain).
Indivisibility	The NFTs can be divided, but the exchange must be carried out in their entirety. Thus, it is not possible to own a portion of an NFT.
Scarcity	NFTs are scarce because there is only ever one NFT that exists.

users, the path to creating an NFT via these platforms usually follows several phases (see, for an example, www.opensea.io).

In the first phase, users typically have to access the selected platform to register an account, create a profile, and establish a "virtual wallet." A personal email address is usually all that is required for this operation. In the second phase, users choose the prospective NFT and the type of file to create or transform (e.g., an image, video, audio, document, and thus images such as Jpg, Png, Gif, videos such as Svg, Mp3, Mp4, Wav, Webm, or documents such as Ogg, Glb, Pdf formats). In the third phase, users are required to provide a name and short description for the digital object, alongside a link to a personal webpage (which can also be one's profile on a social network, a blog, or even a podcast). In the fourth phase, users upload the digital file that will undergo a blockchain-based transformation process (as described below). In the last phase, the NFT is created and the user must define the reward required for payment or the royalties to be deducted from the transaction (generally in the Ether currency, a cryptocurrency alternative of Bitcoin). Afterward, the NFT can be shared, sold, or given away, whether through the platform marketplace or an automatically generated link that can be shared on the major social networks. Once the virtual object is purchased in accordance with the desired rewards (e.g., royalties), the user transfers the NFT and its certified deed to the buyer.

The entire process is illustrated in Fig. 2.1.

2 Blockchain: The Technology Behind NFTs

The main characteristics of NFTs are attributable to the fundamental pillars of the underlying technology: namely, the "Blockchain" (Wang et al., 2021).

A "blockchain" is a distributed ledger technology that has wide applications for registering property, provenance, and authenticity (Whitaker et al., 2021). It consists of a set of software applications that store data in registers that are structured as a chain of blocks (hence, the name). All the completed and authenticated transaction blocks are connected from the beginning of the chain to the most current block. The blockchain allows data to be stored in a fashion that is (O'Dwyer, 2020) transparent (the record is public), decentralized (the contents are transmitted, shared, and collectively verified by all participants, as nodes, in the network), and immutable (because of the cryptographic protocols behind the

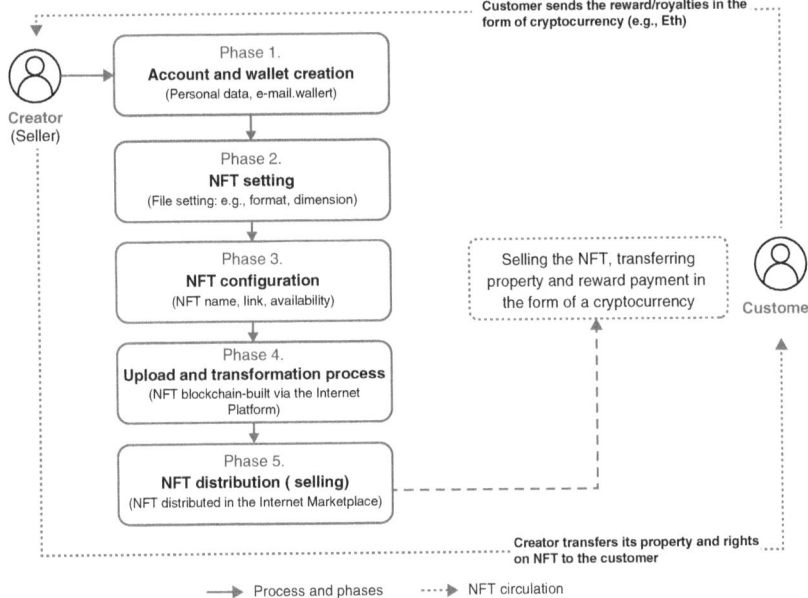

Fig. 2.1 Five phases in the NFT creation process

certification process, it is next to impossible to double-spend or cleanse new transactions in the ledger). Notably, transaction data are distributed across several nodes—that is, copies of the same chain of blocks—of the network (see, for reviews, Gorkhali et al., 2020; Pilkington, 2016).

To better understand these concepts, it is possible to divide the process of data management in a blockchain into seven stages: (1) The creation of data entry in which data (in the form of a transaction) are requested and authenticated; (2) the formation of a block representing the created transaction; (3) the sending of this block to every node (every participant) in the network; (4) the validation of the transaction by the nodes; (5) the sending of the reward/payment to nodes for proofing the chain (inasmuch as all the chain members accept to share and welcome the new contents); (6) the addition of the new block to the existing chain; and, finally, (7) the distribution of the update across the network. Figure 2.2 schematically represents the process of storing data on the blockchain.

In closely analyzing this process, we can observe that the creation of a block is identified and certified with a unique identifier—named

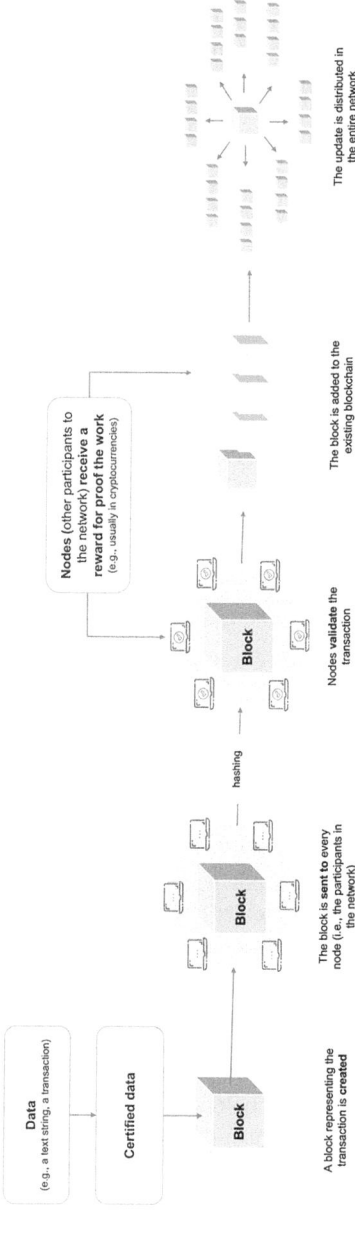

Fig. 2.2 The data management process in the blockchain

"hash"—through the use of suitable (hashing) algorithms that can guarantee the uniqueness of the identified information (Gupta, 2017; Seok et al., 2019). The term "hash" refers to a cryptographic function, consisting of a mathematical algorithm that maps data of a certain type (e.g., data in the form of a message) into a fixed-size binary string called a "hash value" (also known as a "digest"). The uniqueness of this string is what secures the storage of individuals' personal data (Singhal et al., 2018). Through the hash function, any type of string can be transformed into a unique alphanumeric code.

For instance, the word "book," as a text string, may result in a code similar to "ED25FFGS". Such hashes allow one to certify the data and build a block that will form part of the blockchain. Once the data has been certified, the created block is sent to the nodes in the network. The nodes consist of all those computers (and thus, individuals) that are interconnected within the network (Nofer et al., 2017). All the interconnected nodes can participate in the process of validating transactions to be included in the ledger (Maxmudjanovna et al., 2020). On a technical level, the content of the register is transparent and visible to all the members, and it is easily accessible and verifiable. Once written into the register, data cannot be modified without the consensus of the whole network (Pilkington, 2016).

Because of the security it offers to transactions, this process may help in certifying and validating several business applications. Consider that the blockchain results in a chain of blocks, qualified by a special hash, linked and then n-times replicated in the network. Thus, modifying a single block of data signals a required change in the hash that is used to certify the network. Since the block concatenation in the chain is obtained by inserting the previous hash in the block (in the "n - 1" position), any modification is immediately incorporated in all subsequent blocks supplemented the network. Due to the complexity of such an operation and the necessity of simultaneously repeating this change across the entire blockchain, it is nearly impossible to fraudulently modify the chain.

This process guarantees the immutability of the data inserted into the network and allows for countless applications (Saberi et al., 2019; Zhai et al., 2019). To date, the most popular blockchain business applications include those aimed at supply-chain management (Dujak & Sajter, 2019): accurately identifying the position of items in the supply chain, monitoring the quality of products, and helping to prevent losses.

In the FTs' field, their main application is the proposition and management of cryptocurrencies, such as the Bitcoin (Vujičić et al., 2018). Bitcoin was the first "digital" currency built on the concept of blockchain, together with Ether (the cryptocurrency of the Ethereum IT platform). Although both Bitcoin and Ether are based on the blockchain technology, they are quite different in nature and have different uses (Song et al., 2019). Bitcoin was the first to establish a form of currency that is not tied to a central bank or to a specific country (Ciaian et al., 2016; Dwyer, 2015), whereas Ethereum is a ledger technology that companies are using to build new programs—the latter one is much more robust and can be considered as a version 2.0 of the former one, allowing for the creation of decentralized applications to be built on top of it.

There is also a real potential, not only for firms but also for public actors to integrate blockchain-based applications into their activities. For instance, governments could transform digital voting into a blockchain-based transaction whereby a person's vote can be certified as legitimate or during a referendum (Park et al., 2021). In this context, the blockchain can add transparency to the voting process by allowing regulators to immediately notice changes made to the network. Another opportunity is documentary certification, such as accreditations of educational paths and written products. This could apply to scientific research (Shah et al., 2021), property deeds (Themistocleous, 2018), medicines' traceability (Sylim et al., 2018), as well as the development of mobile applications that can enhance end-users' perception of information safety (Sestino et al., 2022). Due to being built around the immutability of information, the blockchain has been recognized as one of the most reliable technologies for perceived data security without the involvement of a central authority.

To summarize, a blockchain system requires the participation of a multitude of users, who merely need to install a special software and be connected to the Internet (Gupta, 2017). As described above, the block becomes available and stored in multiple copies distributed across a large number of computers. When a transaction is made, a message is automatically sent to all connected and active computers in the blockchain. A set of protocols decides which systems are called to process the transaction and add the new block to the chain after generating cryptographic codes (so-called hashing). Shortly after, all the computers participating in the management of the blockchain will synchronize their local copies of the file that contains the chain. From this perspective, the blockchain represents a large shared public ledger whose reliability is extremely high: To falsify information, it would be necessary to break complex cryptography on most of the computers involved in the management process, which is practically impossible.

REFERENCES

Ante, L. (2021). The Non-Fungible Token (NFT) Market and its Relationship with Bitcoin and Ethereum. BRL Working Paper Series, No. 20.

Chohan, R., & Paschen, J. (2021, in press). *What Marketers Need to Know about Non-Fungible Tokens (NFTs)*. Business Horizons. https://doi.org/10.1016/j.bushor.2021.12.004

Ciaian, P., Rajcaniova, M., & Kancs, D. (2016). The Economics of BitCoin Price Formation. *Applied Economics, 48*(19), 1799–1815.

Dujak, D., & Sajter, D. (2019). Blockchain Applications in Supply Chain. In A. Kawa & A. Maryniak (Eds.), *SMART Supply Network* (pp. 21–46). Springer International Publishing.

Durham, J. (1965). Confusion of Fungible and Non-Fungible Goods. *Baylor Literature Review, 17*, 80–89.

Dwyer, G. P. (2015). The Economics of Bitcoin and Similar Private Digital Currencies. *Journal of Financial Stability, 17*(2015), 81–91.

Evans, T. M. (2019). Cryptokitties, Cryptography, and Copyright. *AIPLA QJ, 47*, 219.

Focus. (2021). The First NFT Millionaire Made It Possible for Anyone to Earn $171,000 A Month by Investing. Retrieved January 18, 2022, from https://focus.com.au/first-nft-project-on-opensea

Forbes. (2021). NFTs, Metaverse and GameFi Are Changing Up the Fashion Business in 2022. Retrieved February 2, 2022, from https://www.forbes.com/sites/josephdeacetis/2021/12/22/nfts-metaverse-and-gamefi-are-changing-up-the-fashion-business-in-2022

Gorkhali, A., Li, L., & Shrestha, A. (2020). Blockchain: A Literature Review. *Journal of Management Analytics, 7*(3), 321–343.

Gupta, S. S. (2017). Blockchain: IBM Online. Retrieved December 23, 2021, from http://www.ibm.com

Maxmudjanovna, A. I., Abdurasulovna, P. R., & Erkinovna, N. N. (2020). The Future of the Digital Economy: Concept and Role of Blockchain Technologies. *Journal of Critical Reviews, 7*(8), 1812–1818.

Nadini, M., Alessandretti, L., Di Giacinto, F., Martino, M., Aiello, L. M., & Baronchelli, A. (2021). Mapping the NFT Revolution: Market Trends, Trade Networks, and Visual Features. *Scientific Reports, 11*(1), 1–11.

Nofer, M., Gomber, P., Hinz, O., & Schiereck, D. (2017). Blockchain. *Business & Information. Systems Engineering, 59*(3), 183–187.

O'Dwyer, R. (2020). Limited Edition: Producing Artificial Scarcity for Digital Art on the Blockchain and Its Implications for the Cultural Industries. *Convergence*, 26(4), 874–894.

Oliveira, L., Zavolokina, L., Bauer, I., & Schwabe, G. (2018). To Token Or Not to Token: Tools for Understanding Blockchain Tokens. Retrieved December 28, 2021, from https://www.zora.uzh.ch/id/eprint/157908/

Park, S., Specter, M., Narula, N., & Rivest, R. L. (2021). Going from Bad to Worse: From Internet Voting to Blockchain Voting. *Journal of Cybersecurity*, 7(1), 25–31.

Pilkington, M. (2016). Blockchain Technology: Principles and Applications. In F. X. Olleros & M. Zhegu (Eds.), *Research Handbook on Digital Transformations* (pp. 41–48). Edward Elgar Publishing.

Saberi, S., Kouhizadeh, M., Sarkis, J., & Shen, L. (2019). Blockchain Technology and Its Relationships to Sustainable Supply Chain Management. *International Journal of Production Research*, 57(7), 2117–2135.

Seok, B., Park, J., & Park, J. H. (2019). A Lightweight Hash-Based Blockchain Architecture for Industrial IoT. *Applied Sciences*, 9(18), 3740–3745.

Serada, A., Sihvonen, T., & Harviainen, J. T. (2021). CryptoKitties and the New Ludic Economy: How Blockchain Introduces Value, Ownership, and Scarcity in Digital Gaming. *Games and Culture*, 16(4), 457–480.

Sestino, A., Giraldi, L., Cedrola, E., & Guido, G. (2022). The Relevance of Individuals' Perceived Data Protection Level on Intention to Use Blockchain-Based Mobile Apps. An Experimental Study. In M. Al-Emran (Ed.), *Recent Innovations in Artificial Intelligence and Smart Applications*. Springer International Publishing, in press.

Shah, D., Patel, D., Adesara, J., Hingu, P., & Shah, M. (2021). Exploiting the Capabilities of Blockchain and Machine Learning in Education. *Augmented Human Research*, 6(1), 1–14.

Singh, J., & Singh, P. (2021). Distributed Ownership Model for Non-Fungible Tokens. *Smart and Sustainable Intelligent Systems*, 12, 307–321.

Singhal, B., Dhameja, G., & Panda, P. S. (2018). How Blockchain Works. In B. Singhal, G. Dhameja, & P. S. Panda (Eds.), *Beginning Blockchain* (pp. 31–148). Apress.

Song, J. Y., Chang, W., & Song, J. W. (2019). Cluster Analysis on the Structure of the Cryptocurrency Market via Bitcoin-Ethereum Filtering. *Physica A: Statistical Mechanics and Its Applications*, 527, 121339–121345.

Sylim, P., Liu, F., Marcelo, A., & Fontelo, P. (2018). Blockchain Technology for Detecting Falsified and Substandard Drugs in Distribution: Pharmaceutical Supply Chain Intervention. *JMIR Research Protocols*, 7(9), e10163–e10172.

Themistocleous, M. (2018). Blockchain Technology and Land Registry. *Cyprus Review*, 30(2), 195–202.

Vujičić, D., Jagodić, D., & Ranđić, S. (2018). Blockchain Technology, Bitcoin, and Ethereum: A Brief Overview. In *17th International Symposium INFOTEH-JAHORINA (INFOTEH)*, pp. 1–6.

Wang, Q., Li, R., Wang, Q., & Chen, S. (2021). Non-Fungible Token (NFT): Overview, Evaluation, Opportunities and Challenges. Retrieved December 1, 2021, from https://arxiv.org/abs/2105.07447

Whitaker, A., Bracegirdle, A., de Menil, S., Gitlitz, M. A., & Saltos, L. (2021). Art, Antiquities, and Blockchain: New Approaches to the Restitution of Cultural Heritage. *International Journal of Cultural Policy, 27*(3), 312–329.

Wilson, K. B., Karg, A., & Ghaderi, H. (2021, in press). Prospecting Non-Fungible Tokens in the Digital Economy: Stakeholders and Ecosystem, Risk and Opportunity. Business Horizons.

Wired. (2021). NFT e Musica. Perché Sono Fatti l'Uno per l'Altro? Retrieved October 31, 2021, from https://www.wired.it/play/musica/2021/07/03/nft-musica-funzionano/

Zhai, S., Yang, Y., Li, J., Qiu, C., & Zhao, J. (2019). Research on the Application of Cryptography on the Blockchain. *Journal of Physics: Conference Series, 1168*(3), 032077–032089.

CHAPTER 3

A Review of the Marketing Literature on NFTs

Abstract Given the increasing relevance and popularity of NFTs in online markets, this chapter presents a review of the available marketing literature on this subject. This review adopts a *systematic approach* that combined proper technology-related and business-related keywords to search for relevant papers published on the topic from 2015 to 2021 and available on major academic databases (e.g., Business Source Premiere). Three central topics around NFTs emerged from this literature review—that is, *intellectual property*, *lifestyles*, and *entertainment*—which are widely discussed along with related business opportunities.

Keywords Systematic review on NFTs • Intellectual property • Lifestyles • Entertainment

The above process shows that NFTs can encompass any type of content that can be digitized, such as videos, music, GIFs, 3D objects, images, games, transactions, text, memes, or tweets. Although NFTs have gained relevance as a technology and topic in the last five years (2015–2021), many Internet users remain unfamiliar with this discourse. Web searches for "NFT" as a term only began to increase at the end of 2020, and mostly in the first months of 2021 (see Figs. 3.1 and 3.2). That said, in contrast to related emerging technologies such as Artificial Intelligence (e.g., Brynjolfsson & Mcafee, 2017; Sestino & De Mauro, 2021), Big Data

A. Sestino et al., *Non-Fungible Tokens (NFTs)*, https://doi.org/10.1007/978-3-031-07203-1_3

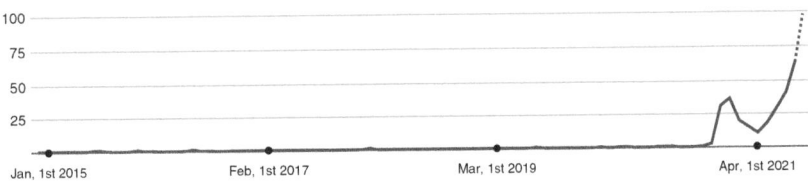

Fig. 3.1 NFTs' term popularity (2015–2021), authors' elaboration of Google Trends data

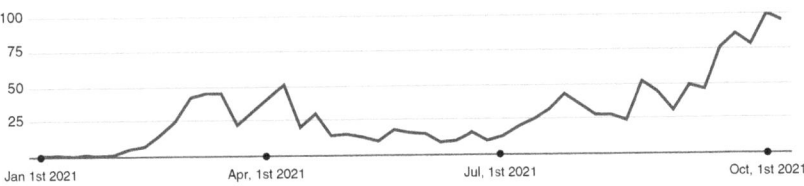

Fig. 3.2 NFTs' term popularity (Jan. 2020–Dec. 2021), authors' elaboration of Google Trends data

(e.g., De Mauro et al., 2019; Erevelles et al., 2016), and Internet of Things (e.g., Nguyen & Simkin, 2017; Sestino et al., 2020), NFTs have become the most popular phenomenon.

Today, interest in NFTs is growing largely through social networks. For instance, TikTok—the notorious video-focused social network—is now incentivizing the exploitation of these unique digital objects and their associated cryptocurrencies. In this context, leading famous creators are beginning to launch their own NFT collections. The rapper Lil Nas X, whose meteoric rise began on TikTok, was the first artist to create NFT-backed musical content on the platform in October 2021; similarly, during the first months of 2021, Jack Dorsey (the creator of Twitter) posted the first NFT-based post, that was sold at the launch of TIPS, the Twitter-hosted platform system consisting of a payment method designed to "make the social network the home of NFT artists" (CNBC, 2021).

Despite this growing attention, knowledge about NFTs remains disorganized and businesses are hazy on how to exploit the associated opportunities. In order to delineate the premise and novelty of NFTs as a new research stream, this chapter aims to provide a systematic review of the existing marketing and consumer literature on NFTs, as well as to introduce a series of empirical studies in those domains where NFTs' business opportunities are rising. With the current review, we seek to organize the few available studies on this topic and to increase researchers and practitioners' knowledge about how NFTs can be used to transform traditional marketing offers in new ones.

1   A Systematic Approach

The novelty of this topic implies that the literature contains few relevant contributions. Nonetheless, we sought to discuss—in a systematic review—the most promising business opportunities and possible applications involving NFTs.

We began our search by defining a list of seven technology-related key-words (i.e., "Non-Fungible Token," "NFT," "token," "tokenization," "blockchain," "digital," "digital object") alongside several business-related key-words (i.e., "advertising," "marketing," "management," "business"), most recurring in scholarly articles on consumers and marketing published in the most important management journals. We carried out a series of queries through combinations of keywords for the considered time range, from 2015 to 2021 (e.g., "Non-Fungible Token" AND "marketing", AND "Pubyear > 2015" AND "Pubyear < 2021"). A sample query was "TITLE-ABS (("Non-fungible" AND "token") and ("business" AND "marketing")) AND PUBYEAR > 2015 AND (LIMIT-TO (DOCTYPE, "ar") OR LIMIT-TO (DOCTYPE, "cp")) AND (LIMIT-TO (LANGUAGE, "English")). We mined the three main business databases (i.e., Business Source Premiere and EconLit, hosted by EBSCO; and ABI/INFORM Complete from ProQuest), as well as double-checked the Google Scholar platform for any other working paper and report, due to the research topic. In order to capture all potentially relevant contributions (both theoretical and experimental ones), we also considered other management and marketing journals that featured research areas related to marketing and consumption (i.e., retailing, communication, market research, services).

We limited the raw data by only considering the last five years (January 1, 2015–December 1, 2021), which reflected the use of the word NFTs in Google searches. We only considered articles published in international scholarly peer-reviewed journals. We then read any article abstract to check its congruence with our research objective. We fully read the text of the final selected contributions, as well as reviewed their references to find other relevant articles that did not emerge from the mining process.

Table 3.1 The emerging topics and the related business opportunities deriving from NFTs

Topics	Main Business Opportunities
Intellectual property	• *Digital artworks* • *Academia* • *Memes and viral contents on the web*
Lifestyles	• *Sports and leisure time* • *Fashion* • *Virtual world*
Entertainment	• *Music and films* • *Videogames* • *Pornography and other "embarrassing products"*

Finally, we contextualized each article's emerging insights in a coherent and integrated manner (as suggested by Bal & Nijkamp, 2001), to get the most comprehensible number of topics in order to capture the most prominent business opportunities related to NFTs' technologies. Then, we grouped the relevant insights and the related contents into three main emerging topics: "Intellectual property," "Lifestyles," and "Entertainment" (see Table 3.1).

2   MAIN TOPICS AND BUSINESS OPPORTUNITIES

2.1   *Intellectual Property*

2.1.1   *Digital Artworks*

NFTs can represent an artwork, a painting, or a patented logo on which one can have intellectual property rights. There are already companies that sell tokens as licenses, which could allow authors to control their creative work and ensure they are paid adequately. One of the most widely known uses of NFTs, in the context of cultural heritage, is the protection and guarantee of artworks, which may encourage the dematerialization and transformation of art itself (Bolton & Cora, 2021).

NFTs assign artworks a digital identity and authenticate their genuine content (Kietzmann et al., 2020). A museum could hypothetically continue to have the right to display an artwork but return ownership rights and payment rights to the source country (Whitaker et al., 2021). The owner of each specific right would be immutably recorded in the blocks on the chain. On a prospective basis, the blockchain can also be used to register artwork objects at the point of discovery on archeological digs, leading to much greater clarity around future ownership and provenance. These blockchain-enabled approaches can respectfully contribute to questions of identity, heritage, authorship, and cross-cultural definitions of property. Moreover, blockchain can be used to discourage the sale of looted artworks and manage the shared stewardship, ownership, and exhibition of these contested artifacts. For artists, the blockchain technology provides an opportunity to protect their work from illegal licensing and expropriation (O'Dwyer, 2020).

This technology is easily applied to "digital" artworks, too. "CryptoPunks," for examples, is a collection of 10,000 uniquely generated characters with proof of ownership stored on the Ethereum blockchain (Schaar & Kampakis, 2022). All CryptoPunks are 24 × 24-pixel art images that were inspired by cyberpunk. When the CryptoPunks collection was released, all characters could be claimed for free. Since all of them were claimed very quickly, they can now be traded via the OpenSea marketplace, where it is possible to offer, bid on, and purchase such artworks. The main benefit for the art market is a higher transparency since all activities are publicly available. The blockchain also allows the decoupling of ownership and exhibition rights, as well as the assignment of shared ownership and shared revenues. Other parties, such as micro-donor members of the public, could purchase tokens related to an artistic project and potentially receive tax deductions or other benefits. Blockchain technology allows reintroducing the notions of authenticity, originality, and scarcity into freely reproducible digital artworks (O'Dwyer, 2020). Nowadays, some of the most prosperous examples of blockchain and digital art are collectibles that blur the boundaries between art and asset.

By purchasing an NFT-based artwork, consumers essentially buy a virtual document: namely, a "smart contract" that certifies their right to possess the work itself (Bsteh & Vermeylen, 2021). The artwork is made available online through its digital copy (i.e., a digital object), which consists of a photo, a video, or a painting, in digital form (Rae, 2021). In this sense, NFTs represent unique and inimitable virtual objects, as their development and production are certified and traced at each stage according to the blockchain technology on which NFTs are developed.

2.1.2   Academia

NFTs also present implications for intellectual property rights in academia. For instance, UC Berkeley was the first university to employ NFTs to certify and disclose two patents (i.e., the CRISPR-Cas9 for gene editing and cancer immunotherapy). NFTs allowed researchers to certify the authorship of their inventions, as well as sell the university patent disclosure form for an amount of 22 ETH (Ether, at that time, was equal to 55,000 dollars).

Given their characteristics, NFTs enable numerous opportunities for patent management. Indeed, their technicalities, in terms of immutability and uniqueness, are able to unfold the usefulness of these tools in combating violations of the individual property (Bamakan et al., 2022). Thus, not only can the patents be registered at the competent offices of the various nations around the world but also they can be built on the basis of the NFT technology certifying their absolute uniqueness and the licensee's intellectual property (Barakat et al., 2022). In December 2021, for example, IBM decided to turn to IPwe—that is, a platform offering information and tools to companies to identify, research, evaluate, and transact their patents (which has long been approaching the world of intellectual property with cutting-edge tools, including the use of artificial intelligence for the evaluation of patents)—to exploit NFT technologies for the creation, management, and sale of intellectual property outputs, thus proposing a new ways of registering patents and trademarks (Agenda Digitale, 2022).

2.1.3   Memes and Viral Contents on the Web

In recent years, "memes" have proliferated across the Web and social media, in particular. A *meme* is a piece of digital, and often humorous, content that spreads rapidly across the Internet, thanks to sharing behavior on social networks (Shifman, 2013). Most memes utilize photos (or videos) with captions, intended to arouse hilarity, usually taken from some television show or movie. In this context, the concept of "Meme Marketing" represents a growing effort to integrate memes into brand marketing and advertising campaigns (Zhang & Huang, 2021), with the ultimate goal of increasing attention around a brand (Sharma, 2018; Wu & Ardley, 2007). Because of memes' rapid spread, it can be useful for creators—who are usually anonymous and unpaid—to be able to link themselves to their creations (Panda & Palejwala, 2020). In this context, NFTs offer an unprecedented marketing opportunity, as they can certify and ensure the authorship and possession of viral Web contents (Sharma, 2018). Not surprisingly, one of the most popular memes of 2020—namely, "Disaster girl," which portrays a little girl smirking in front of a burning house—was auctioned off in its original digital version for a value of 180 Ether, which amounted to almost 170,000 dollars (BBC, 2021). This opportunity could be magnified when meme creators are businesses whose marketing strategy entails using the meme's popularity to drive interest in the brand (Sharma, 2018; Wu & Ardley, 2007).

2.2   Lifestyles

2.2.1   Sports and Leisure Time

The opportunities deriving from NFTs' technology are slowly penetrating the sphere of consumers' lifestyles, particularly in relation to sports and fashion (e.g., Raman & Benson, 2021). One of the first segments to experiment in this regard was the sneakers market, where consumers are generally more attentive to news and inclined to collect unique products (Business of Fashion, 2021). Obviously, given the peculiarities of the fashion market, it is clear that not all brands are ready for virtual experiments of this magnitude. Sports enthusiasts have always been interested in the collectibles of their heroes and of their favorite teams (Kosík, 2011): thus, NFTs, given their characteristics, lend themselves perfectly to digital collections. Sports-themed NFTs are another greater marketing opportunity. In the same way that leagues sell licensed clothing, video games, cards, action figures, and memorabilia, NFTs represent another class of e-commerce, with many more potential applications in sports (Wang et al., 2021).

This type of innovation will soon be led by the athletes themselves, who are becoming more and more multimedia celebrities also thanks to social networks (Deloitte, 2022): The players' unions, large and small, have made great strides in recent years to help stars to monetize themselves separately from their teams. Interestingly, recently Warner Media's "Bleacher Report" sold a limited series of digital basketballs in connection with a celebrity event that took place during the NBA "All-Star Weekend" (Sportico, 2021).

Furthermore, like other physical objects that can be transformed into digital items, NFTs may be one of the elements that will give greater value to physical tickets and collectibles (Wang et al., 2021). Summarizing, from stickers to digital video, NFTs today bring sports memorabilia and leisure time items into the digital age.

2.2.2   Fashion

In fashion or luxury industries, traditional customers are less familiar with virtual environments and only recently have becoming acquainted in their goals of purchase, such as the search for status or personal pleasure (Amatulli & Guido, 2012; Guido et al., 2020), with product innovations.

NFTs are all the rage, and for brands, they pose unforeseen opportunities: Fashion brands have recently been studying the wild, wacky world of the blockchain and all its creative and business possibilities, and are now poised to join in (Tripathi et al., 2021; Wilson et al., 2021). In recent months, the fashion industry has finally embraced the NFTs' opportunities (Forbes, 2021): Numerous fashion houses have begun to produce virtual copies of their collections (e.g., dresses, shoes, and so on) that can be shown off and worn exclusively in the virtual world (The Guardian, 2021). A new, parallel, unique, and original market is born also in the field of fashion. On these digital channels, products that are impossible to duplicate and wear in reality can be purchased, unique for those who wear them and, therefore, able—by their nature—to offer a feeling of greater satisfaction or to demonstrate one's status to others as well (O'Cass & McEwen, 2004). This new scenario is now known as CyberFashion, in which designer skins take hold or virtual copies of real clothes offered by fashion houses such as Dior, Nike, Balenciaga. These copies skillfully contribute to personalizing their virtual characters, that is, their avatars, making them almost identical to real ones. Consistently, Dolce & Gabbana auctioned a fine luxury dress for more than a million dollars (Vogue, 2021); about 620 pairs of sneakers, produced by RTFKT Studios and designed by Fewocious, generated sales for three million dollars in just seven minutes (OpenSea, 2021); and the Baby Birkin bag, produced by Hermes and decorated by Mason Rothschild and Eric Ramirez, auctioned off for the equivalent of a cool $23,500 (Vogue Business, 2021). Incredibly, despite the huge value, none of these products "really" exist and are only virtually showable.

The collaboration through shared values of innovation and pioneering, launched in 2019 between Louis Vuitton and the League of Legends during the world championships in Paris, may also represent another interesting case study for e-games (Louis Vuitton, 2022): A bespoke travel case for the Summoner's Cup trophy was directly designed by Nicolas

Ghesquiere, the artistic director of Louis Vuitton women's collections, along with other digital assets, including some pieces of NFTs and a digital collection of clothing for players.

The numerous fashion brands that appear on these digital platforms are now willing to invest in virtual clothing, giving life to specialized marketplaces in the sector, such as "Digitalax" (www.digitalax.xyz) on which they propose their customized lines that take on the competitive role of the brands of standard luxury. Additional platforms, as in the case of "Exclusible," rank as premium, curated NFTs' marketplaces designed for luxury brands across the verticals of fashion, beauty, watches, jewelry, lifestyle, and supercars. In these platforms, not only NFT-based clothing but also accessories, such as glasses, bags, hats, sneakers, etc., are sold and virtually worn on the Web.

These digital items generated as NFTs are purchased at considerable amounts and the related properties of intangibility often clash with the fervent desire of prospective buyers to be able to show them off in reality (Bolton & Cora, 2021).

2.2.3   Virtual World

NFTs have numerous implications in a "virtual world" (Ahmad & Abdulkarim, 2019). A virtual world—technically a "Massively Multiplayer Online World" (MMOW)—is a computer-simulated environment that is colonized by numerous virtual users. These users may create personal avatars who can "really" live in that parallel world, thus exploring that virtual world, participating in its activities, and communicating with other virtual inhabitants (Girvan, 2018). These avatars may be textually or graphically represented and can perform commercial transactions, thanks to virtual currencies such as Ether. One example is Decentraland (MANA), which provides a virtual reality platform based on the Ethereum blockchain (Chaudhari et al., 2019). In this digital world, users can spend their daily lives attending live musical performances, shopping, buying virtual goods, and even driving, having lifestyles which can be completely different from theirs in reality (Laskowski-Jones, 2020).

With their characteristics, NFTs represent the ideal typical objects that can be purchased in these virtual worlds (Wang et al., 2021). For example, it is already possible to buy unique artworks or clothing that can be displayed in one's virtual home or at virtual parties (Business of Fashion, 2021). As mentioned above, Gucci, for instance, has proposed virtual sneakers—called the *Gucci 25*—which, once purchased, can be only displayed in virtual worlds or through the augmented reality features of mobile devices.

2.3   Entertainment

2.3.1   Music and Films

NFTs are currently revolutionizing the entertainment sector: from music, to movies, and so on. Music is a field which in recent years has undergone significant transformations in terms of distribution to the public, passing from old vinyls (which have never completely disappeared from the market) to CDs and, then, to streaming (Bartmanski & Woodward, 2018). With the advent of the NFTs, four things immediately became evident. First, during the COVID-19 pandemic, music artists (e.g., singers, musicians) were financially hurt by the disruption of their public-facing activities, such as shows and concerts. In this context, NFTs represent a new way for musicians to generate income. By anchoring a music file to NFT-based tokens, musicians can gain greater control over their productions while developing closer relationships with their fans (Musictech, 2021). Second, the blockchain makes it easy to verify the authenticity of a music file, which grants the current owner more credibility when reselling (Goanta, 2020). Third, the possible elimination of intermediaries (e.g., physical music stores) empowers artists to sell directly to the market. Fourth, NFTs allow artists to potentially receive royalties in the case of a resale. In Italy, for example, a singer, Morgan, has auctioned a piece of his own music to the highest bidder, who can then become the exclusive owner for a share of 10 Ether (about 21,000 dollars). Similarly, Belladonna, an Italian music band, proposed a unique piece of their new single entitled "New future travelogue," becoming the first artist in Italy to sell a single copy of a piece as an NFT; they were also the first in the world to include the rights to that song in the sold NFT (Wired, 2021). This means that the highest-bidding consumer won not only the sole copy of that piece of music as an NFT, thus becoming its owner, but also the rights related to that song, such as collecting royalties from streaming platforms.

Another promising NFT-related opportunity involves the film industry. In cinema, it is possible to link film scenes to NFTs in order to render them unique, collectible, and purchasable on appropriate marketplaces (e.g., OpenSea or Crypto.com platforms). Technically, it is possible to "tokenize" films in small frames, by recording their metadata (hence their attributes) on a series of Ethereum blockchain chains (AGI, 2021). This concept is already being tested with the film *Zero Contact*, a thriller starring Anthony Hopkins that has been launched on a new platform dedicated to NFTs, named "Vuele." This platform aims to create scarcity in copies of the film in order to guard against piracy and guarantee a greater sense of uniqueness for the owners. More recently, also the Oscar-winner director Quentin Tarantino has tried to sell some NFTs picturing famous scenes taken from his movies for millions of dollars, thus arousing the opposite reaction of the Miramax production company which claimed to own the rights to such scenes (Lee, 2022).

2.3.2   Videogames

A different important business opportunity which is materializing from the diffusion of NFTs is related to the videogame industry (Chevet, 2018; Mortensen, 2007; Serada et al., 2021). In this case, NFTs can serve as digital collectibles or game props, such as weapons, clothing, and other items. Instead of game creators relying on centralization, security, and validation, they can maintain digital scarcity using decentralized blockchain technology. Indeed, as mentioned above, the first applications of NFTs came from the world of games: namely, "CryptoKitties" (Evans, 2019). In this game, players buy and breed digital cats that can then be traded as figurines through NFTs. The game found enormous success, with some digital kittens reaching values up to 170,000 dollars (Wired, 2021). The opportunities multiply when applied to online events such as races, battles, and fights between players in mainline videogames. On such occasions, winners of in-game events may obtain a special reward for their achievement: a unique NFT that will no longer be released within the game itself, the possession of which will signify a victory for life (Forbes, 2022).

2.3.3   Pornography and Other "Embarrassing Products"

Since the advent of the Internet, the adult entertainment industry has been quick to adopt technological innovations (Stewart & Zhao, 2000). Appropriately, numerous companies and creators have already begun experimenting with NFTs. Similar to other industries, the pornography industry has approached the world of NFTs as a way to not only provide their customers with unique content but also solve long-standing issues such as counterfeiting or the inability to upload pornographic content to certain social networks (Johnson, 2010; Rodeschini, 2021).

Indeed, sex workers have always struggled to maintain a presence on large social platforms, where they are often shadowed or banned altogether for minimal violations of content guidelines (Coletto et al., 2017; Gehl, 2021). As such, some of them see NFTs as a way of diversifying their income, while ensuring that no one can eliminate their content (The Guardian, 2021). As an example of such practices, the RarePorn platform was the first to adapt NFTs' technology to redirect the adult content industry, among other things by collecting significant funding from the initiative, attested to around 5.8 billion dollars (Rolling Stone, 2021). Similarly, Brazzers, a Canadian pornographic production house, announced its entry into the world of blockchain by proposing the "Brazzers 420 Collection": an assortment of adult content (in video and image formats) available on the NFT marketplace. Likewise, PornVisory decided to expand into the NFTs' industry via an adult trading card game, which was planned to be released in the final quarter of 2021 (Rogers, 2020).

NFTs can be also a tool to support the purchase of products related to the porn or sex industry (such as condoms or sex toys), which are usually considered "embarrassing products" for arousing emotions of discomfiture in those who buy them (Gabler et al., 2004; Londono et al., 2017). The literature shows that consumers are more willing to purchase such intimate products via online environments (i.e., on e-commerce multi-brand and multiproduct platforms, such as Amazon) than offline ones (Sestino et al., 2021). Thus, ironically, NFTs can be a way to bring safety sex and enjoyment also in the virtual world!

3   Three Empirical Studies on Art, Music, and Fashion

NFTs certify the authenticity and uniqueness of owned digital objects. Therefore, someone can become the exclusive owner of a video, an image, a song, and even a virtual good (e.g., computer-generated sneakers, clothes). This new trend is a byproduct of the blockchain technology, which many consider one of the most revolutionary technologies of recent years. Due to the unforeseen success of the blockchain, companies are beginning to see NFTs as a useful promotional vehicle—one that can align their brands with unique and collectible digital items. In this scenario, the value propositions of NFTs can have various potential effects on marketing and advertising strategies: NFTs could become a new tool for creating more attractive marketing campaigns that leverage the technology's ability to foster perceptions of uniqueness and scarcity. One recent example is Burger King's "Keep It Real Meals" campaign, wherein customers could purchase one of the three menus curated by three pop artists (e.g., the singers Nelly, Anitta, and LilHuddy) and receive a QR code—a two-dimensional symbol (as a two-dimensional matrix barcode) composed of black modules arranged within a white square pattern, generally used to store information intended to be read through a special optical reader or even a smartphone (Coleman, 2011)—that granted them a collectible NFT element of a game. By completing various parts of the collection, customers can obtain various gadgets and prizes and possibly exchange their NFTs with other players.

Companies interested in selling their virtual products by using the NFTs' technology could develop appropriate marketing strategies aimed at leveraging the technological characteristics of NFTs by guaranteeing consumers the perception (or the real benefit) of being the only owners of such products. This perception, in turn, could arouse feelings of satisfaction in consumers. In this context, some consumer-related variables could play a fundamental role in marketing strategies, by influencing consumers' acceptance and willingness to buy NFT-based products. Three variables seem to play a key role according to the previous review of the scholarly literature. The first variable—and most recurring one—is *materialism* (Belk, 1985, 1988; Eastman et al., 1997), which is defined as individuals' tendency to consider material possessions and physical comfort as more important than spiritual values. The second one is *status consumption orientation*, which is defined as a behavioral tendency to value status and acquire and consume products that provide prestige to the individual (O'Cass & McEwen, 2004). The third variable is consumers' *innovativeness*, that is, their desire to be among the first to try or buy certain new products (Hoffman et al., 2010; Steenkamp & Gielens, 2003). These three variables seem to influence the targeted consumption choices, thus allowing people to project their extended self into our increasingly digital environment, as preconized by Belk's (2013) theory (see the Introduction to this volume).

In order to investigate both the role and the extent of these variables in the NFTs' market, the next three chapters will present as many empirical studies in which each of these variables has been the main focus, by using as many different settings, that is, respectively: Art (Chap. 4), music (Chap. 5), and fashion (Chap. 6). Results will be discussed in the final chapter, together with implications for marketing theory and practice, limitations and future research aimed to shed light on the variables that shape individuals' consumption choices in response to NFT-based product communications.

REFERENCES

Agenda Digitale. (2022). NFT and Intellectual Property: This Is How the Blockchain Supports the Protection of Rights. Retrieved March 8, 2022, from https://www.agendadigitale.eu/documenti/nft-e-proprieta-intellettuale-ecco-come-la-blockchain-supporta-la-tutela-dei-diritti

AGI. (2021). Che C'Entra la Blockchain con Picasso: A Cosa Servono gli NFT. Retrieved December 12, 2021, from https://www.agi.it/economia/news/2021-03-26/cosa-sono-nft-a-cosa-servono-11920239/

Ahmad, N., & Abdulkarim, H. (2019). The Impact of Flow Experience and Personality Type on the Intention to Use Virtual World. *International Journal of Human–Computer Interaction, 35*(12), 1074–1085.

Amatulli, C., & Guido, G. (2012). Externalized vs. Internalized Consumption of Luxury Goods: Propositions and Implications for Luxury Retail Marketing. *The International Review of Retail, Distribution and Consumer Research, 22*(2), 189–207.

Bal, F., & Nijkamp, P. (2001). In Search of Valid Results in a Complex Economic Environment: The Potential of Meta-analysis and Value Transfer. *European Journal of Operational Research, 128*(2), 364–384.

Bamakan, S. M. H., Nezhadsistani, N., Bodaghi, O., & Qu, Q. (2022). Patents and Intellectual Property Assets as Non-Fungible Tokens: Key Technologies and Challenges. *Scientific Reports, 12*(1), 1–13.

Barakat, S., Yaghi, K., & Al-Zagheer, H. (2022). The Use of NFT for Patent Protection. *Advances in Dynamical Systems and Applications, 17*(1), 107–113.

Bartmanski, D., & Woodward, I. (2018). Vinyl Record: A Cultural Icon. *Consumption Markets & Culture, 21*(2), 171–177.

BBC. (2021). Side-Eyeing Chloe' Clem to Sell Iconic Meme as NFT. Retrieved March 12, 2022, from https://www.bbc.com/news/world-us-canada-58659667

Belk, R. W. (1985). Materialism: Trait Aspects of Living in the Material World. *Journal of Consumer Research, 12*(3), 265–280.

Belk, R. W. (1988). Possessions and the Extended Self. *Journal of Consumer Research, 15*(2), 139–168.

Belk, R. W. (2013). Extended Self in a Digital World. *Journal of Consumer Research, 40*(3), 477–500.

Bolton, S. J., & Cora, J. R. (2021). Virtual Equivalents of Real Objects (VEROs): A Type of Non-Fungible Token (NFT) that Can Help Fund the 3D Digitization of Natural History Collections. *Megataxa, 6*(2), 93–95.

Brynjolfsson, E., & Mcafee, A. (2017). Artificial Intelligence, for Real. *Harvard Business Review, 1*, 1–31.

Bsteh, S., & Vermeylen, F. (2021). From Painting to Pixel: Understanding NFT Artworks. Retrieved December 18, 2022, from http://www.researchgate.net/publication/351346278_From_Painting_to_Pixel_Understanding_NFT_artworks

Business of Fashion. (2021). The State of Fashion 2021 Report: Finding Promise in Perilous Times. Retrieved January 8, 2022, from https://www.businessoffashion.com/reports/news-analysis/the-state-of-fashion-2021-industry-report-bof-mckinsey/

Chaudhari, A. A., Laddha, D., & Potdar, M. (2019). Decentraland: A Blockchain-Based Model for Smart Property Experience. *International Engineering Journal for Research & Development, 4*(5), 5–15.

Chevet, S. (2018). Blockchain Technology and Non-Fungible Tokens: Reshaping Value Chains in Creative Industries. Retrieved December 12, 2021, from https://papers.ssrn.com/sol3/papers.cfm?abstract_id=3212662

CNCB. (2021). I Kind of Freaked Out': This 42-year-old Artist Made Over $738K in 32 minutes Selling. Retrieved at: https://www.cnbc.com/2022/03/13/this-42-year-old-artistmade-over-738k-in-32-minutes-selling-nfts.html. Accessed on the June 6th 2022.

Coleman, J. (2011). QR Codes: What Are They and Why Should You Care? *Kansas Library Association College and University Libraries Section Proceedings, 1*, 16–23.

Coletto, M., Aiello, L. M., Lucchese, C., & Silvestri, F. (2017). Adult Content Consumption in Online Social Networks. *Social Network Analysis and Mining, 7*(1), 1–21.

De Mauro, A., Greco, M., & Grimaldi, M. (2019). Understanding Big Data Through a Systematic Literature Review: The ITMI Model. *International Journal of Information Technology & Decision Making, 18*(04), 1433–1461.

Deloitte. (2022). From Trading Cards to Digital Video: Sports NFTs Kick Sports Memorabilia into the Digital Age. Retrieved March 5, 2022, from https://www2.deloitte.com/xe/en/insights/industry/technology/technology-media-and-telecom-predictions/2022/sports-nfts-digital-media.html

Eastman, J. K., Fredenberger, B., Campbell, D., & Calvert, S. (1997). The Relationship Between Status Consumption and Materialism: A Cross-Cultural Comparison of Chinese, Mexican, and American Students. *Journal of Marketing Theory and Practice, 5*(1), 52–66.

Erevelles, S., Fukawa, N., & Swayne, L. (2016). Big Data Consumer Analytics and the Transformation of Marketing. *Journal of Business Research, 69*(2), 897–904.

Evans, T. M. (2019). Cryptokitties, Cryptography, and Copyright. *AIPLA QJ, 47,* 219.

Forbes. (2021). NFTs, Metaverse and GameFi Are Changing Up the Fashion Business in 2022. Retrieved February 2, 2022, from https://www.forbes.com/sites/josephdeacetis/2021/12/22/nfts-metaverse-and-gamefi-are-changing-up-the-fashion-business-in-2022

Forbes. (2022). Why Video Game Makers See Huge Potential in Blockchain – And Why Problems Loom for Their New NFTs. Retrieved March 14, 2022, from https://www.forbes.com/sites/justinbirnbaum/2022/01/06/why-video-game-makers-see-huge-potential-in-blockchain-and-why-problems-loom-for-their-new-nfts/?sh=7be09e3b43d7

Gabler, J., Kropp, F., Silvera, D. H., & Lavack, A. M. (2004). The Role of Attitudes and Self-Efficacy in Predicting Condom Use and Purchase Intentions. *Health Marketing Quarterly, 21*(3), 63–78.

Gehl, R. W. (2021). Dark Web Advertising: The Dark Magic System on Tor Hidden Service Search Engines. *Continuum, 35*(5), 1–12.

Girvan, C. (2018). What Is a Virtual World? Definition and Classification. *Educational Technology Research and Development, 66*(5), 1087–1100.

Goanta, C. (2020). Selling LAND in Decentraland: The Regime of Non-Fungible Tokens on the Ethereum Blockchain under the Digital Content Directive. In A. Lehavi & R. Levine-Schnur (Eds.), *Disruptive Technology, Legal Innovation, and the Future of Real Estate* (pp. 139–154). Springer International Publishing.

Guido, G., Amatulli, C., Peluso, A. M., De Matteis, C., Piper, L., & Pino, G. (2020). Measuring Internalized versus Externalized Luxury Consumption Motivations and Consumers' Segmentation. *Italian Journal of Marketing, 4*(1), 1–23.

Hoffman, D. L., Kopalle, P. K., & Novak, T. P. (2010). The "Right" Consumers for Better Concepts: Identifying Consumers High in Emergent Nature to Develop New Product Concepts. *Journal of Marketing Research, 47*(5), 854–865.

Johnson, J. A. (2010). To Catch a Curious Clicker: A Social Network Analysis of the Online Pornography Industry. In K. Boyle (Ed.), *Everyday Pornography* (pp. 22–43). Routledge.

Kietzmann, J., Lee, L. W., McCarthy, I. P., & Kietzmann, T. C. (2020). Deepfakes: Trick Or Treat? *Business Horizons, 63*(2), 135–146.

Kosík, M. (2011). Marketing Strategy in Connection with Sport. *Marketing, 7*(2), 92–98.

Laskowski-Jones, L. (2020). Living and Dying in a Virtual World. *Nursing, 50*(7), 6–15.

Lee, E. (2022). NFTs as Decentralized Intellectual Property, SSRN. Retrieved December 14, 2022, from https://papers.ssrn.com/sol3/papers.cfm?abstract_id=4023736

Londono, J. C., Davies, K., & Elms, J. (2017). Extending the Theory of Planned Behavior to Examine the Role of Anticipated Negative Emotions on Channel Intention: The Case of an Embarrassing Product. *Journal of Retailing and Consumer Services, 36*, 8–20.

Louis Vuitton. (2022). Louis Vuitton Collection for League of Legends. Retrieved March 6, 2022, from https://it.louisvuitton.com/ita-it/magazine/articoli/league-of-legends-collection

Mortensen, T. E. (2007). Mutual Fantasy Online: Playing with People. In J. P. Williams & J. H. Smith (Eds.), *The Players' Realm: Studies on the Culture of Video Games and Gaming* (pp. 188–211). Jefferson, NC.

Musictech. (2021). Artists Are Selling Their Music as NFTs – And They're Making Millions. Retrieved December 21, 2021, from https://www.musictech.net/news/artists-selling-music-nft-making-millions/

Nguyen, B., & Simkin, L. (2017). The Internet of Things (IoT) and Marketing: The State of Play, Future Trends and the Implications for Marketing. *Journal of Marketing Management, 33*(1-2), 1–6.

O'Cass, A., & McEwen, H. (2004). Exploring Consumer Status and Conspicuous Consumption. *Journal of Consumer Behaviour, 4*(1), 25–39.

O'Dwyer, R. (2020). Limited Edition: Producing Artificial Scarcity for Digital Art on the Blockchain and Its Implications for the Cultural Industries. *Convergence, 26*(4), 874–894.

OpenSea. (2021). OpenSea: Browse NFT. Retrieved March 8, 2022, from https://opensea.io/assets

Panda, S., & Palejwala, D. A. (2020). Effectiveness of Meme Marketing. Retrieved December 13, 2021, from https://repository.iimb.ac.in/handle/2074/19460

Rae, M. (2021). Analyzing the NFT Mania: Is a JPG Worth Millions? In *SAGE Business Cases*. SAGE Publications, Ltd. Retrieved July 17, 2021, from https://doi.org/10.4135/9781529779332

Raman, R., & Benson, E. R. (2021). The World of NFTs (Non-Fungible Tokens): The Future of Blockchain and Asset Ownership. In B. M. Adel & L. Chaari Fourati (Eds.), *Enabling Blockchain Technology for Secure Networking and Communications* (pp. 89–108). IGI Global.

Rodeschini, S. (2021). New Standards of Respectability in Contemporary Pornography: Pornhub's Corporate Communication. *Porn Studies, 8*(1), 76–91.

Rogers, S. (2020). PornVisory Lays Out Its Blockchain Future. Retrieved December 22, 2021, from https://gritdaily.com/pornvisory-blockchain-future/

Rolling Stone. (2021). Rolling Stone and Coinbase Are Collaborating with 12 Artists on an Exclusive NFT Drop. Retrieved November 28, 2021, from https://www.rollingstone.com/culture/culture-features/rolling-stone-and-coinbase-nft-drop-1292861/

Schaar, L., & Kampakis, S. (2022). Non-Fungible Tokens as an Alternative Investment: Evidence from CryptoPunks. *The Journal of the British Blockchain Association, 5*(1), 31949–31959.

Serada, A., Sihvonen, T., & Harviainen, J. T. (2021). CryptoKitties and the New Ludic Economy: How Blockchain Introduces Value, Ownership, and Scarcity in Digital Gaming. *Games and Culture, 16*(4), 457–480.

Sestino, A., & De Mauro, A. (2021). Leveraging Artificial Intelligence in Business: Implications, Applications and Methods. *Technology Analysis & Strategic Management, 34*(1), 16–29.

Sestino, A., Prete, M. I., Piper, L., & Guido, G. (2020). Internet of Things and Big Data as Enablers for Business Digitalization Strategies. *Technovation, 98*(C), 102173–102181.

Sestino, A., Prete, M. I., Piper, L., & Guido, G. (2021). The Future of Online Marketing Strategies and Digital Tools: New Challenges and Contribution to the RACE Framework. *International Journal of Electronic Trade.* https://doi.org/10.1504/IJETRADE.2021.10042594

Sharma, H. (2018). Memes in Digital Culture and Their Role in Marketing and Communication: A Study in India. *Interactions: Studies in Communication & Culture, 9*(3), 303–318.

Shifman, L. (2013). Memes in a Digital World: Reconciling with a Conceptual Troublemaker. *Journal of Computer-Mediated Communication, 18*(3), 362–377.

Sportico. (2021). NFT Boom Leaves a Crypto or Cash Conundrum for Teams and Athlete. Retrieved March 8, 2022, from https://www.sportico.com/business/finance/2021/sports-nft-sales-crypto-1234629061/

Steenkamp, J. B. E., & Gielens, K. (2003). Consumer and Market Drivers of the Trial Probability of New Consumer Packaged Goods. *Journal of Consumer Research, 30*(3), 368–384.

Stewart, D. W., & Zhao, Q. (2000). Internet Marketing, Business Models, and Public Policy. *Journal of Public Policy & Marketing, 19*(2), 287–296.

The Guardian. (2021). A Virtual Steal: The Digital Gucci Sneakers for Sale at $17.99. Retrieved November 11, 2021, from https://www.theguardian.com/fashion/2021/mar/19/a-virtual-steal-the-gucci-sneakers-for-sale-at-1799

Tripathi, G., Tripathi Nautiyal, V., Ahad, M. A., & Feroz, N. (2021). Blockchain Technology and Fashion Industry-Opportunities and Challenges. *Blockchain Technology: Applications and Challenges, 12*(19), 201–220.

Vogue. (2021). Dolce & Gabbana Porta gli NFT nel Mondo della Moda. Retrieved December 30, 2022, from https://www.vogue.it/moda/article/dolce-gabbana-ntf-haute-couture-moda-venezia

Vogue Business. (2021). The 'Baby Birkin' NFT and the Legal Scrutiny on Digital Fashion. Retrieved January 30, 2022, from https://www.voguebusiness.com/technology/the-baby-birkin-nft-and-the-legal-scrutiny-on-digital-fashion

Wang, Q., Li, R., Wang, Q., & Chen, S. (2021). Non-Fungible Token (NFT): Overview, Evaluation, Opportunities and Challenges. Retrieved December 1, 2021, from https://arxiv.org/abs/2105.07447

Whitaker, A., Bracegirdle, A., de Menil, S., Gitlitz, M. A., & Saltos, L. (2021). Art, Antiquities, and Blockchain: New Approaches to the Restitution of Cultural Heritage. *International Journal of Cultural Policy, 27*(3), 312–329.

Wilson, K. B., Karg, A., & Ghaderi, H. (2021, in press). Prospecting Non-Fungible Tokens in the Digital Economy: Stakeholders and Ecosystem, Risk and Opportunity. Business Horizons.

Wired. (2021). NFT e Musica. Perché Sono Fatti l'Uno per l'Altro? Retrieved October 31, 2021, from https://www.wired.it/play/musica/2021/07/03/nft-musica-funzionano/

Wu, Y., & Ardley, B. (2007). Brand Strategy and Brand Evolution: Welcome to the World of the Meme. *The Marketing Review, 7*(3), 301–310.

Zhang, T., & Huang, X. (2021). Viral Marketing: Influencer Marketing Pivots in Tourism: A Case Study of Meme Influencer Instigated Travel Interest Surge. *Current Issues in Tourism, 10*, 1–8.

CHAPTER 4

How Materialism Influences the Purchase of NFT-Based Artworks

Abstract This chapter proposes the notion that *materialism* (i.e., the individuals' tendency to appreciate material possessions more than spiritual values) could be a major determinant of consumers' intention to purchase NFT-based digital products. Thus, it presents an empirical study that tests this notion in a virtual artworks' setting. The obtained results provided evidence for this notion by showing a positive relationship between materialism and consumers' intention to purchase NFT-based artworks.

Keywords Art setting • NFT-based products • Materialism • Consumers' purchase intention

1 INTRODUCTION

Art and culture represent a considerable part of Western countries' economies. As a result, marketing scholars have turned their attention to these topics to stimulate a certain response among various audience members, who are often drawn to unconventional artistry (Colbert, 2003). When properly managed, marketing and advertising strategies can bolster the artistic component by facilitating its spread and, by extension, its value.

In this scenario, marketing aesthetics revolves around all those subjects of the artistic and cultural world (e.g., individual artists, cultural institutions, museums, and other organizations) that offer their independent work to the marketplace while maintaining their autonomy (Venkatesh & Meamber, 2006). In this domain, the scope of marketing embraces not only the creation of an artistic product that is stimulating and pleasant to consumers but also the definition of appropriate promotional campaigns and the identification of the adequate pricing, production, distribution, and sales policies for the selected market segment (Bourgeon-Renault, 2000; Colbert, 2003). Marketers and managers need to understand customer orientations in order to plan and implement campaigns capable of attracting the attention of target markets. At their most effective, marketers in the artistic and cultural sector must position artworks so that they can capture the experiences, expectations, and desires of the public (Colbert, 2003).

Of course, digitization has permeated this sector like any other. Now, marketers and managers have unprecedented opportunities to promote and sell artistic offerings online (Zhou, 2018), as well as to integrate new digital technologies useful to guide consumers in the use of artistic works, as it happens in museums (e.g., Panciroli et al., 2017).

Against this backdrop, NFTs represent a potential revolution in the artistic context thanks to the unique form of ownership they can confer over an artwork. Indeed, individuals do not generally buy an artwork simply to appreciate its cultural value (Kleine & Baker, 2004); the act of material possession also satisfies their own need for status and desire for consumption (Eastman et al., 1997; Richins, 2004). Given these premises, the present study investigates the determinant role of materialism in consumers' purchase intention toward an advertised artwork developed within the NFTs' technology.

2   THEORETICAL BACKGROUND

Similar to the luxury goods market, the consumption of artworks mainly relies on the construct of materialism and, in turn, ostentation (Belk, 1985; Richins & Dawson, 1992). In many occasions, people use art to signal their status and social position to others (Amatulli & Guido, 2011, 2012; Guido et al., 2020; Peluso et al., 2017). *Materialism* has been defined as a system of personal values oriented toward the acquisition of specific goods that are essential to achieving a desired state and a fundamental mediator in the event of product deriving from emerging economies (Demirbag et al., 2010). For materialists, the purchase and consumption of goods can positively influence their satisfaction (Ger & Belk, 1996). Highly materialistic people tend to place greater value on products that can be shown to others (such as luxury items or personal collections). These consumers often seek to feel kinship with a group or be recognized for certain characteristics, which can help them maintain or improve their own social status (O'Cass & McEwen, 2004). Indeed, several studies have considered materialism to be a relevant factor in consumption (Eastman et al., 1997), whereby individuals view goods as central to their values (Chang & Arkin, 2002; Richins & Dawson, 1992) and a symbolic expression of their desire to belong to an upper class (Vigneron & Johnson, 2004).

According to Richins and associates (Richins, 2004; Richins & Dawson, 1992), materialism features three dimensions—that is, success, centrality, and happiness—which can drive consumers toward purchasing and owning certain products (e.g., luxury products) in an attempt to show off their status and social position to others. Similarly, materialism could be a critical determinant of consumers' purchase intentions of artworks. This could be especially true for digital artworks whose main benefit is their possession and display in a virtual environment. Therefore, a marketing campaign designed to advertise digital artworks should leverage on this psychological factor by activating in consumers a sense of materially "possessing" such digital objects (i.e., acquiring them to reach the desired higher status). This sense of exclusive propriety seems particularly critical when such artworks are based on NFT technologies. Indeed, without such technologies, the ownership of such immaterial products could not be certified in front of everyone. Therefore, we proposed the following hypothesis (see Fig. 4.1):

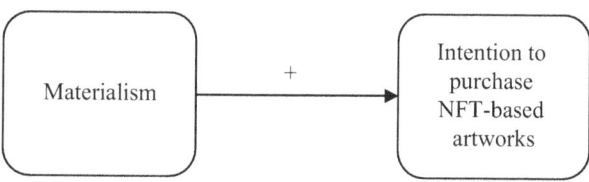

Fig. 4.1   The influence of materialism on consumers' intention to purchase NFT-based artworks

Hp: Materialism is positively related to consumers' intention to purchase NFT-based artworks.

3   METHODOLOGY

To test our hypothesis, we carried out a survey study by administering a structured questionnaire to a sample of 94 international respondents. Subjects were recruited online via Amazon's Mechanical Turk, a crowd-sourcing platform widely used by social scientists for research purposes (Aguinis et al., 2021).

First, respondents were asked to indicate their level of materialism by using nine items adapted from Richins (2004) (i.e., "I admire people who own expensive homes, cars, and clothes," "The things I own say a lot about how well I'm doing in life," "I like to own things that impress people," "I try to keep my life simple, as far as possessions are concerned," "Buying things gives me a lot of pleasure," "I like a lot of luxury in my life," "My life would be better if I owned certain things I don't have," "I'd be happier if I could afford to buy more things," "It sometimes bothers me quite a bit that I can't afford to buy all the things I'd like") and assessed on a seven-point Likert scale (1 = "Strongly disagree," 7 = "Strongly agree").

In the second part of the questionnaire, respondents were presented with a scenario in which they saw an ad message regarding a digital artwork produced using a complex design software. Respondents read that they could purchase, download, and store that artwork online through an NFT technology, which would have certified that they would have been the unique owners of that artwork. Following that, respondents indicated their intention to purchase that artwork by using three items adapted from Dodds et al. (1991) (i.e., "I would buy the advertised artwork," "I would consider buying the advertised artwork," "The probability that I would consider buying the advertised artwork is high") and assessed on a seven-point Likert scale (1 = "Strongly disagree," 7 = "Strongly agree").

Finally, in the third part of the questionnaire, respondents provided sociodemographic information about their age, gender, education level, and nationality.

4   RESULTS

4.1   Sample Description

The sample used for this study comprised 94 respondents with an average age of 35.15 years (SD = 9.87); 54.3% of them were men and 45.7% were women. Regarding their education level, 18.1% held a high-school diploma and 81.9% held a bachelor's or master's degree. Most respondents lived in the United States (44.7%) and Europe (44.7%), with minor portions living in Canada (7.4%), India (2.1%), and China (1.1%).

4.2   Descriptive and Reliability Statistics

The key constructs assessed in the survey were *materialism* and *purchase intention*, which were measured using two multi-item scales. The nine items assessing materialism were checked for internal consistency by computing Cronbach's alpha index (α = 0.88). This index was greater than the recommended threshold of 0.60 (Hair et al., 2013), thus confirming the internal consistency of the scale. Therefore, we averaged the scores obtained on such nine items to constitute an aggregate measure of *materialism* (M = 5.69, SD = 0.88).

We followed the same procedure for the three items assessing willingness to purchase (Cronbach's α = 0.38). As the alpha index for this construct was below the aforementioned recommended threshold, we inspected each of the three items assessing intention to purchase in order to identify potentially unreliable items. A correlation analysis showed that the first two items (i.e., "I would buy the advertised artwork" and "I would consider buying the advertised artwork") were strongly interrelated (r = 0.77, p < 0.001), whereas the third one (i.e., "The probability that I would consider buying the advertised artwork is high") was not significantly correlated with each of the first two items (p values $\geq$ 0.30). Therefore, for this study, we removed the latter item and retained the first two. Thus, we averaged the scores obtained on the first two items to constitute an aggregate measure of respondents' intention to purchase the advertised artwork (M = 6.06, SD = 0.94).

4.3   Hypothesis Testing

To test our hypothesis, we estimated a linear regression model that expressed respondents' intention to purchase the advertised artwork as a function of their level of materialism, while statistically controlling for their age, gender (coded as a binary variable taking the value 1 = female and 0 = male), and education level (1 = high school diploma, 2 = bachelor's or master's degree, 3 = doctoral degree). As hypothesized, the obtained results revealed a relationship between materialism and purchase intention that was positive and significant ($b = 0.55$, $p < 0.001$), while no significant relationship emerged between the three socio-demographic variables and the dependent variable (p values > 0.25) (see Table 4.1).

5   DISCUSSION AND IMPLICATIONS

In this study, we explored the role of materialism in determining consumers' intention to purchase digital artworks based on NFT technologies.

While material possession related to "real" goods has been a long-debated issue (e.g., Belk, 1985, 1988; Vigneron & Johnson, 1999), academic research has only recently considered the material possession of "digital" goods, suggesting that consumers attach less value to digital products than to physical ones (Atasoy & Morewedge, 2018). Framed differently, individuals would be willing to pay more for tangible goods than equivalent digital goods (e.g., souvenir photographs, books, films). Tangible goods are generally ascribed higher value because of their greater overlap between physical and psychological possession. However, with the

Table 4.1 Results of the regression analysis showing the role of materialism in determining purchase intention

Independent variable	b	SE	Beta	t	p
Constant	2.53	0.81		3.14	0.002
Age	0.01	0.01	0.06	0.68	0.501
Gender	0.15	0.17	0.08	0.89	0.377
Education level	0.06	0.23	0.02	0.25	0.800
Materialism	0.55	0.10	0.52	5.77	< 0.001

Note: $N = 94$. Dependent variable: Intention to purchase the advertised artwork. Gender coded as 1 = female and 0 = male. Education level coded as 1 = high school diploma, 2 = bachelor's or master's degree, 3 = doctoral degree. Fit statistics: $R = 0.53$, $R^2 = 0.28$, Adjusted $R^2 = 0.25$, Std. error of the estimate = 0.82, $F(4, 93) = 8.64$, $p < 0.001$

advent of NFTs, materialism might play a critical role also in the possession of digital goods. Indeed, unlike other digital goods, NFT-based products offer a certified ownership and the potential for a unique digital possession (Wang et al., 2021). Such features can alter consumers' purchase intentions toward this type of products. Consistent with this view, our results indicate that consumers' level of materialism predicts their willingness to buy NFT-based products—and, particularly, artworks.

Our study contributes to the consumption literature by suggesting that materialistic individuals—for example, some luxury buyers—can be relatively more inclined to purchase NFT-based products insofar as this technology allows them to experience a sense of ownership and unique possession similar to that felt for "real" products. Our findings is also compatible with the notion that materialistic consumers might buy digital products not only for "externalized motives," in an attempt to reach or reinforce their social status (Guido et al., 2020), but also for "internalized" reasons, whereby individuals are mainly motivated by their desire to experience intimate feelings and emotions, as when they enjoy the fact that they—and only "they"—can get and claim the ownership of an artwork. As a consequence, advertising messages regarding digital artworks and other products using NFTs should emphasize the sense of unique ownership connected with this technology, thus increasing a sense of originality and exclusivity in consumers.

Future studies could enrich this emerging stream of literature by investigating the role of other consumer characteristics. Additionally, research could consider whether an NFT-based artwork can influence consumers' perception of some specific characteristics—whether in terms of unicity, prestige, rarity, and other elements. In this way, digital companies could be provided with relevant insights on how to restructure their consumer value propositions around new digital tools to succeed in our hyperconnected world.

References

Aguinis, H., Villamor, I., & Ramani, R. S. (2021). MTurk Research: Review and Recommendations. *Journal of Management, 47*(4), 823–837.

Amatulli, C., & Guido, G. (2011). Determinants of Purchasing Intention for Fashion Luxury Goods in the Italian Market: A Laddering Approach. *Journal of Fashion Marketing and Management, 15*(1), 123–136.

Amatulli, C., & Guido, G. (2012). Externalized vs. Internalized Consumption of Luxury Goods: Propositions and Implications for Luxury Retail Marketing. *The International Review of Retail, Distribution and Consumer Research, 22*(2), 189–207.

Atasoy, O., & Morewedge, C. K. (2018). Digital Goods Are Valued Less Than Physical Goods. *Journal of Consumer Research, 44*(6), 1343–1357.

Belk, R. W. (1985). Materialism: Trait Aspects of Living in the Material World. *Journal of Consumer Research, 12*(3), 265–280.

Belk, R. W. (1988). Possessions and the Extended Self. *Journal of Consumer Research, 15*(2), 139–168.

Bourgeon-Renault, D. (2000). Evaluating Consumer Behaviour in the Field of Arts and Culture Marketing. *International Journal of Arts Management, 3*(1), 4–18.

Chang, L., & Arkin, R. M. (2002). Materialism as an Attempt to Cope with Uncertainty. *Psychology & Marketing, 19*(5), 389–406.

Colbert, F. (2003). Entrepreneurship and Leadership in Marketing the Arts. *International Journal of Arts Management, 6*(1), 30–39.

Demirbag, M., Sahadev, S., & Mellahi, K. (2010). Country Image and Consumer Preference for Emerging Economy Products: The Moderating Role of Consumer Materialism. *International Marketing Review, 27*(2), 141–163.

Dodds, W. B., Monroe, K. B., & Grewal, D. (1991). Effects of Price, Brand, and Store Information on Buyers' Product Evaluations. *Journal of Marketing Research, 28*(3), 307–319.

Eastman, J. K., Fredenberger, B., Campbell, D., & Calvert, S. (1997). The Relationship Between Status Consumption and Materialism: A Cross-Cultural Comparison of Chinese, Mexican, and American Students. *Journal of Marketing Theory and Practice, 5*(1), 52–66.

Ger, G., & Belk, R. W. (1996). Cross-cultural Differences in Materialism. *Journal of Economic Psychology, 17*(1), 55–77.

Guido, G., Amatulli, C., Peluso, A. M., De Matteis, C., Piper, L., & Pino, G. (2020). Measuring Internalized versus Externalized Luxury Consumption Motivations and Consumers' Segmentation. *Italian Journal of Marketing, 4*(1), 1–23.

Hair, J. F., Black, W. C., Babin, B. J., & Anderson, R. E. (2013). *Multivariate Data Analysis.* Pearson.

Kleine, S. S., & Baker, S. M. (2004). An Integrative Review of Material Possession Attachment. *Academy of Marketing Science Review, 1*(1), 1–39.

O'Cass, A., & McEwen, H. (2004). Exploring Consumer Status and Conspicuous Consumption. *Journal of Consumer Behaviour, 4*(1), 25–39.

Panciroli, C., Russo, V., & Macauda, A. (2017). When Technology Meets Art: Museum Paths Between Real and Virtual. *Multidisciplinary Digital Publishing Institute Proceedings, 9*(1), 913–927.

Peluso, A. M., Pino, G., Amatulli, C., & Guido, G. (2017). Luxury Advertising and Recognizable Artworks: New Insights on the "Art Infusion" Effect. *European Journal of Marketing, 51*(11/12), 2192–2206.

Richins, M. L. (2004). The Material Values Scale: Measurement Properties and Development of a Short Form. *Journal of Consumer Research, 31*(1), 209–219.

Richins, M. L., & Dawson, S. (1992). A Consumer Values Orientation for Materialism and Its Measurement: Scale Development and Validation. *Journal of Consumer Research, 19*(3), 303–316.

Venkatesh, A., & Meamber, L. A. (2006). Arts and Aesthetics: Marketing and Cultural Production. *Marketing Theory, 6*(1), 11–39.

Vigneron, F., & Johnson, L. W. (1999). A Review and a Conceptual Framework of Prestige-Seeking Consumer Behavior. *Academy of Marketing Science Review, 1*(1), 1–15.

Vigneron, F., & Johnson, L. W. (2004). Measuring Perceptions of Brand Luxury. *Journal of Brand Management, 11*(6), 484–506.

Wang, Q., Li, R., Wang, Q., & Chen, S. (2021). Non-Fungible Token (NFT): Overview, Evaluation, Opportunities and Challenges. Retrieved December 1, 2021, from https://arxiv.org/abs/2105.07447

Zhou, H. (2018). Characteristics of User Experience in Art E-commerce: Case "Buybuy Art". Retrieved November 28, 2021, from https://trepo.tuni.fi/handle/10024/103861

The Roles of Materialism and Status Consumption Orientation in the Purchase of NFT-Based Music Compilations

Abstract This chapter suggests the notion that, in addition to *materialism* (i.e., the individuals' tendency to appreciate material possessions more than spiritual values), *status consumption orientation* (i.e., the individuals' tendency to consume products that confer them a sense of prestige) could be another determinant of consumers' intention to purchase NFT-based digital objects. Thus, it presents an empirical study that tests this notion in a music setting. While the obtained results confirmed the determinant role of materialism, they also provided preliminary evidence for a positive relationship between status consumption orientation and consumers' intention to purchase NFT-based products.

Keywords Music setting • NFT-based products • Materialism • Status consumption orientation • Consumers' purchase intention

1 INTRODUCTION

Music is one of humanity's most long-standing means of communication and pleasure, due to its ability to evolve alongside social, cultural, environmental, and technological shifts (Masataka, 2007). Fittingly, the world of music is already being tangibly affected by digitization, which has significant implications for marketing strategies (Fuentes et al., 2019).

© The Author(s), under exclusive license to Springer Nature Switzerland AG 2022
A. Sestino et al., *Non-Fungible Tokens (NFTs)*,
https://doi.org/10.1007/978-3-031-07203-1_5

In the last decades, the music industry has undergone a progressive decline due to digitization diminishing the barriers to duplicating and exchanging musical content (Bataille & Perrenoud, 2021). Indeed, in the history of the media music system, two great technological periods may be conventionally distinguished: the first, which goes from the end of the nineteenth century to the 1980s of the twentieth Century, namely "Analogical," and the second, which goes from the 1980s to the present, namely "Digital" (Fouce-Rodríguez, 2010).

Toward the end of the 1970s, thanks to laser reading technology, work began on the creation of a distribution system for digital recordings—that is, the compact discs (CD-ROMs)—which was launched on the Japanese market and, then, in the rest of the world in the late 1980s (Immink, 1998). The next phase in the digitization of post-CD music was marked by the appearance of MP3, in 1993, as a compressed format—virtually audible but recorded on a physical device—that exploited hypo-acoustic phenomena to reduce the amount of data necessary to reproduce a record: The size of the compressed file could reach over one-tenth of those of the original file and transmission times by telematics could be considerably reduced. Marketing strategies, consequently, evolved in an attempt to satisfy the rapid changes stimulated by the new technological advances (Ogden et al., 2011). CD-ROMs, which often represented original collectible products containing consumer favorite music, such as older pieces of vinyl, began to give way to content that could be used without the support of a real physical object (Hogg & Jackson, 2009). Indeed, the music industry moved away from old media, such as pieces of vinyl and CD magnetic tapes, in favor of new dematerialized forms. The shelves full of collectible CD-ROMs, that once embodied the possession of original objects—also signable by the artists—with an extreme, intrinsically sentimental value on the part of the collectors, were replaced by virtual libraries, available in mobile apps on smartphones (Odom et al., 2011). Since then, music has gone "liquid": today consumers have a very large library of songs in their devices that can be accessed anywhere and at any time, immediately usable via an Internet connection (Fuentes et al., 2019; Stafford, 2010).

All in all, in the last decade, the music supply chain has experienced a profound disintermediation (Waldfogel, 2017). People, nowadays, can access music from digital platforms like Spotify, stream from social media networks, play songs through their smartphones' Bluetooth capabilities, and purchase tunes directly from artists' websites. Against this backdrop, some artists have embraced NFT-based technologies in an attempt to offer unique musical pieces in a new digital format which guarantees exclusive ownership. Similarly, marketers have tried to get advantages from these technological changes and improve their advertising strategies.

In the following study, we tried to integrate the results from the previous chapter and investigate the possible influence of consumers' *status consumption orientation*, in addition to that of *materialism*, as a related but distinct predictor of the intention to purchase NFT-based music compilations available on the Internet.

2   THEORETICAL BACKGROUND

When it comes to studying the influence of new technologies on consumption, one should consider that there are certain individuals who like to buy and to show off to others any novelty the market could offer them in terms of new products and services. To highly materialistic consumers, the pleasure they derive may relate less to satisfying their personal needs and more to simply owning and flaunting their goods to others (Cleveland & Chang, 2009; Eastman et al., 1997; Guido et al., 2020). From this perspective, materialism reflects a value that is capable of influencing individuals' life choices, behaviors, and consumptions (Belk, 1985; Richins, 1994).

Materialism (as defined in the previous chapter), therefore, relates to individuals' *status consumption orientation*, that is, "the behavioral tendency to value status and acquire and consume products that provide status to the individual" (O'Cass & McEwen, 2004, p. 34). Both concepts align in their implication that consumption preferences are mainly dictated by social needs (e.g., ostentation, or sense of belonging). Indeed, the literature has demonstrated that individuals' materialism is positively correlated with the purchase of products that reflect status (Goldsmith & Clark, 2012). In such cases, people derive satisfaction from the public's reaction rather than their own use of products (Wong, 1997).

Status consumption orientation is influenced by consumers' self-monitoring—that is, the consumers' tendency to enhance their overall image in social contexts (O'Cass & Frost, 2002). In line with this reasoning, O'Cass and McEwen (2004) have emphasized that status consumption orientation is "a matter of consumers' desires to gain prestige from the acquisition of status-laden products and brands" (p. 27). Accordingly, Eastman et al. (1999) considered status consumption orientation as an interest in consuming and purchasing to signal owning a status to others. According to this point of view, consumers characterized by high status consumption orientation would get satisfaction mainly from the audience reaction to their possession of a specific product or their display of a certain purchasing power.

In the music market, for example, consumers might buy CDs and vinyl records not only for the purpose of listening to their favorite music but also to collect copies and various compilations of their music idols. By possessing such objects, they would signal their "fan" status to others (Fairchild, 2006). Accordingly, we predicted that music advertising focused on NFTs' technology can tap into this mentality: namely, by certifying the ownership of a musical artifact through the blockchain (Goanta, 2020). In this way, NFTs' technologies may enhance the relationship between music idols and fans. Indeed, anchoring a music file to an NFT delivers several benefits for both artists and consumers: For instance, the former ones can provide the latter ones with unique, authentic files without intermediaries (Musictech, 2021). Not surprisingly, some artists are already moving in this direction, using NFTs to give consumers exclusive pieces of digital music that can accompany a real copy of their musical work (Arcos, 2018). On the other hand, by purchasing NFT-based music files, consumers can perceive themselves as the sole owners of such files (i.e., that only they will be able to own such files unless they sell them). This perception might lead such consumers to pursue these unique virtual copies to satisfy a personal desire for status in addition to their materialistic values. In other words, consumers who have the possibility to buy NFT-based music compilations might be likely to do so driven by their tendency to materialistically possess original pieces of music as well as by their desire to signal their status to others by showcasing such a (rare) type of possession (Cleveland & Chang, 2009; Richins, 2004). Formally, we hypothesized that (see Fig. 5.1):

Hp: Materialism and status consumption orientation are positively related to consumers' intention to purchase NFT-based music compilations.

3   METHODOLOGY

To test our hypothesis, we conducted a survey study by administering a structured questionnaire to a sample of 92 international respondents, who were recruited online via Amazon's Mechanical Turk. They were asked to indicate their level of materialism, by using nine items adapted from

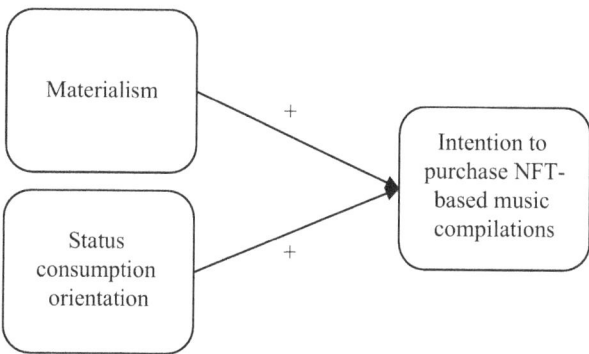

Fig. 5.1 The influence of materialism and status consumption orientation on consumers' intention to purchase NFT-based music compilations

Richins (2004) (e.g., "I admire people who own expensive items, cars, and clothes"), and their level of status consumption orientation, by using five items adapted from Eastman et al. (1999)—that is, "I would buy a product just because it has status," "I am interested in new products with status," "I would pay more for a product if it had status," "The status of a product is relevant to me," and "A product is more valuable to me if it has some snob appeal." Responses on these two sets of items were rated on seven-point Likert scales (1 = "Strongly agree," 7 = "Strongly disagree").

In the second part of the questionnaire, subjects were presented with a scenario in which they saw an ad message regarding a music compilation that was produced using a complex recording software and sold through an NFT-based technology, which would have allowed the purchaser to be the sole owner of that compilation. Afterward, respondents indicated their intention to purchase that product by using three items adapted from Dodds et al. (1991) (e.g., "I would buy the advertised music compilation") and assessed on a seven-point Likert scale (1 = "Strongly disagree," 7 = "Strongly agree"). Finally, respondents provided sociodemographic data regarding their age, gender, education level, and nationality.

4   RESULTS

4.1   Sample Description

The sample comprised 92 respondents with an average age of 35.71 years (SD = 11.69); 56.5% of them were men and 43.5% were women. Regarding their education level, 33.7% held a high-school diploma, 64.1% held a bachelor's or master's degree, and 2.2% held a doctoral degree. Most respondents lived in Europe (33.7%) and the United States (27.1%); the others lived in China (15.2%), Canada (12%), and India (12%).

4.2   Descriptive and Reliability Statistics

Multi-item scales assessing relevant constructs were checked for internal consistency by computing Cronbach's alpha index. This index was adequate for each of the three multi-item scales (*materialism*: $\alpha = 0.80$; *status consumption orientation*: $\alpha = 0.80$; *purchase intention*: $\alpha = 0.85$), thus confirming their internal consistency. Therefore, for each scale, we averaged the scores obtained on the respective items to constitute an aggregate measure of the corresponding construct (*materialism*: $M = 5.19$, $SD = 0.96$; *status consumption orientation*: $M = 5.42$, $SD = 1.11$; *purchase intention*: $M = 5.30$, $SD = 1.33$).

4.3   Hypothesis Testing

We estimated a linear regression model that expressed respondents' intention to purchase the NFT-based music compilation as a function of their level of materialism and level of status consumption orientation, while statistically controlling for their age, gender (coded as a binary variable taking the value 1 = female and 0 = male), and education level (1 = lower than high school, 2 = high-school diploma, 3 = bachelor's or master's degree, 4 = doctoral degree).

Although materialism and status consumption orientation were significantly interrelated ($r = 0.65$, $p < 0.001$), the statistical analysis returned variance inflation factor coefficients below 1.8, thus smaller than the recommended threshold of 10 (Hair et al., 2013), excluding relevant multicollinearity problems.

The obtained results revealed a relationship between materialism and purchase intention that was positive and significant ($b = 0.85$, $p < 0.001$); the relationship between status consumption orientation and purchase intention was positive but marginally significant ($b = 0.22$, $p = 0.065$). No significant relationship emerged between the three socio-demographic variables and the dependent variable (p-values > .35) (see Table 5.1).

Table 5.1 Results of the regression analysis showing the roles of materialism and status consumption orientation in determining purchase intention

Independent Variable	b	SE	Beta	t	p
Constant	-0.49	0.83		-0.59	0.553
Age	-0.01	0.01	-0.07	-0.91	0.366
Gender	0.08	0.20	0.03	0.43	0.667
Education level	0.17	0.19	0.06	0.87	0.385
Materialism	0.85	0.13	0.61	6.40	< 0.001
Status consumption orientation	0.22	0.12	0.18	1.87	0.065

Note: $N = 92$. Dependent variable: Intention to purchase the advertised music compilation. Gender coded as 1 = female and 0 = male. Education level coded as 1 = lower than high school, 2 = high-school diploma, 3 = bachelor's or master's degree, 4 = doctoral degree. Fit statistics: $R = 0.74$, $R^2 = 0.54$, Adjusted $R^2 = 0.52$, Std. error of the estimate = 0.92, $F(5, 91) = 20.48$, $p < 0.001$

5   Discussions and Implications

In this study, we investigated the roles of materialism and status consumption orientation in determining the consumers' intention to purchase NFT-based music compilations.

The advent of NFTs' technology in the music industry has the potential to revolutionize consumers' experience with music. By tokenizing their musical works via NFTs, artists can certify their music as unique, transfer its ownership, and decide to make as many certified copies as they wish. At the same time, NFTs lend consumers new possibilities to collecting material objects that contain music files (CD, vinyl, etc.), the very essence of consumption (Kwong & Park, 2008). Such possessions might be driven by consumers' materialistic values (Belk, 1985; Guido et al., 2016; Kleine & Baker, 2004; Odom et al., 2010) and their desire to seek status (Eastman et al., 1997; Goldsmith & Clark, 2012).

Consistent with our prediction, our findings suggested that materialism and, to a lesser extent, status consumption orientation could be at the basis of a consumer's intention to buy NFT-based music compilations. Such findings carry both theoretical and managerial implications.

Theoretically, they contribute to the research stream on music consumption by exploring the role of materialism in consumers' tendency to purchase music products that, even if digital, may confer a sense of possession to purchasers. Moreover, they show that, albeit conceptually related, materialism and status consumption orientation could serve as independent antecedents of consumers' intention to buy NFT-based pieces of music. Operationally, advertising strategies regarding this type of virtual products could emphasize the key characteristics of NFTs' technology (e.g., uniqueness, authenticity, exclusivity) in order to convert materialistic and status-seeking consumers into actual buyers of NFT-based music products.

Future studies could consider additional individual characteristics which might contribute to explaining in greater detail consumers' intentions toward NFT-based products. Studies on individual differences could be helpful to better understand the effect of status consumption orientation, which was only marginally significant in this investigation. This is what we tried to do in the next chapter, delving deeper into this effect and exploring the role of innovativeness, as another potentially relevant interactive variable in explaining consumers' reaction to NFT-based products available on the Internet.

References

Arcos, L. C. (2018). The Blockchain Technology on the Music Industry. *Brazilian Journal of Operations & Production Management, 15*(3), 439–443.

Bataille, P., & Perrenoud, M. (2021). "One for the Money"? The Impact of the "Disk Crisis" on "Ordinary Musicians" Income: The Case of French Speaking Switzerland. *Poetics, 86*, 1–13.

Belk, R. W. (1985). Materialism: Trait Aspects of Living in the Material World. *Journal of Consumer Research, 12*(3), 265–280.

Cleveland, M., & Chang, W. (2009). Migration and Materialism: The Roles of Ethnic Identity, Religiosity, and Generation. *Journal of Business Research, 62*(10), 963–971.

Dodds, W. B., Monroe, K. B., & Grewal, D. (1991). Effects of Price, Brand, and Store Information on Buyers' Product Evaluations. *Journal of Marketing Research, 28*(3), 307–319.

Eastman, J. K., Fredenberger, B., Campbell, D., & Calvert, S. (1997). The Relationship Between Status Consumption and Materialism: A Cross-Cultural Comparison of Chinese, Mexican, and American Students. *Journal of Marketing Theory and Practice, 5*(1), 52–66.

Eastman, J. K., Goldsmith, R. E., & Flynn, L. R. (1999). Status Consumption in Consumer Behavior: Scale Development and Validation. *Journal of Marketing Theory and Practice, 7*(3), 41–52.

Fairchild. (2006). Fun and Easy Project. Retrieved November 12, 2021, from https://acnpsearch.unibo.it/journal/2255104

Fouce-Rodríguez, H. (2010). Technologies and Media in Digital Music: From Music Market Crisis to New Listening Practices. *Revista Comunicar, 17*(34), 65–71.

Fuentes, C., Hagberg, J., & Kjellberg, H. (2019). Soundtracking: Music Listening Practices in the Digital Age. *European Journal of Marketing, 53*(3), 483–503.

Goanta, C. (2020). Selling LAND in Decentraland: The Regime of Non-Fungible Tokens on the Ethereum Blockchain under the Digital Content Directive. In A. Lehavi & R. Levine-Schnur (Eds.), *Disruptive Technology, Legal Innovation, and the Future of Real Estate* (pp. 139–154). Springer International Publishing.

Goldsmith, R. E., & Clark, R. A. (2012). Materialism, Status Consumption, and Consumer Independence. *The Journal of Social Psychology, 152*(1), 43–60.

Guido, G., Amatulli, C., Peluso, A. M., De Matteis, C., Piper, L., & Pino, G. (2020). Measuring Internalized versus Externalized Luxury Consumption Motivations and Consumers' Segmentation. *Italian Journal of Marketing, 4*(1), 1–23.

Guido, G., Prete, M. I., Pichierri, M., Pino, G., & Peluso, A. M. (2016). *Beyond Ethical Consumption: Religious-like Behaviours and Marketing Habits for Fervid Attachment to Brands.* Peter Lang.

Hair, J. F., Black, W. C., Babin, B. J., & Anderson, R. E. (2013). *Multivariate Data Analysis.* Pearson.

Hogg, N., & Jackson, T. (2009). Digital Media and Dematerialization: An Exploration of the Potential for Reduced Material Intensity in Music Delivery. *Journal of Industrial Ecology, 13*(1), 127–146.

Immink, K. A. (1998). The Compact Disc Story. *Journal of the Audio Engineering Society, 46*(5), 458–465.

Kleine, S. S., & Baker, S. M. (2004). An Integrative Review of Material Possession Attachment. *Academy of Marketing Science Review, 1*(1), 1–39.

Kwong, S. W., & Park, J. (2008). Digital Music Services: Consumer Intention and Adoption. *The Service Industries Journal, 28*(10), 1463–1481.

Masataka, N. (2007). Music, Evolution and Language. *Developmental Science, 10*(1), 35–39.

Musictech. (2021). Artists Are Selling Their Music as NFTs – And They're Making Millions. Retrieved December 21, 2021, from https://www.musictech.net/news/artists-selling-music-nft-making-millions/

O'Cass, A., & Frost, H. (2002). Status Brands: Examining the Effects of Non-Product-Related Brand Associations on Status and Conspicuous Consumption. *Journal of Product & Brand Management, 11*(2), 67–88.

O'Cass, A., & McEwen, H. (2004). Exploring Consumer Status and Conspicuous Consumption. *Journal of Consumer Behaviour, 4*(1), 25–39.

Odom, W., Zimmerman, J., & Forlizzi, J. (2010). Virtual Possessions. In: Proceedings of the 8th ACM Conference on Designing Interactive Systems, Aarhus, Denmark, August 16-2, 368–371.

Odom, W., Zimmerman, J., & Forlizzi, J. (2011). Teenagers and Their Virtual Possessions: Design Opportunities and Issues. In *Proceedings of the International Conference on Human Factors in Computing Systems*, Vancouver, Canada, May 7–12, pp. 1491–1500.

Ogden, J. R., Ogden, D. T., & Long, K. (2011). Music Marketing: A History and Landscape. *Journal of Retailing and Consumer Services, 18*(2), 120–125.

Richins, M. L. (1994). Special Possessions and the Expression of Material Values. *Journal of Consumer Research, 21*(3), 522–533.

Richins, M. L. (2004). The Material Values Scale: Measurement Properties and Development of a Short Form. *Journal of Consumer Research, 31*(1), 209–219.

Stafford, S. A. (2010). Music in the Digital Age: The Emergence of Digital Music and Its Repercussions on the Music Industry. *The Elon Journal of Undergraduate Research in Communications, 1*(2), 112–120.

Waldfogel, J. (2017). How Digitization Has Created a Golden Age of Music, Movies, Books, and Television. *Journal of Economic Perspectives, 31*(3), 195–214.

Wong, N. Y. (1997). Suppose You Own the World and No One Knows? Conspicuous Consumption, Materialism and Self. *Advances in Consumer Research, 24*, 197–203.

CHAPTER 6

The Interplay of Consumer Innovativeness and Status Consumption Orientation When Buying NFT-Based Fashion Products

Abstract This chapter investigates the potential interactive effect of *consumers' innovativeness* (i.e., their desire to be among the first to try or buy a new product) and *status consumption orientation* (i.e., their tendency to consume products that confer them a sense of prestige) on their intention to purchase NFT-based products. The chapter presents an empirical study that tests this effect in a fashion setting. The obtained results showed that consumer innovativeness is positively related to this intention. Furthermore, this construct significantly moderates the effect of status consumption orientation such that the impact of the latter construct on consumers' intention to purchase NFT-based fashion products is positive and significant *only* for innovative consumers.

Keywords Fashion setting • NFT-based products • Consumer innovativeness • Status consumption orientation • Consumers' purchase intention

1   INTRODUCTION

In recent years, new technologies have allowed fashion industry companies to better understand their customers in the B2C market—thus, creating engaging experiences within their physical stores and improving customer relationships in both the online and offline environments

(Amatulli et al., 2021; Lynch & Barnes, 2020; Sestino et al., 2021a). Empowered by the Internet and related advancements like Artificial Intelligence, these technologies represent an ideal tool for marketing managers who want to redesign their production and supply processes (Sestino et al., 2020), consumption experiences (Balaji & Roy, 2017), and the overall shopping experience (Hoyer et al., 2020). Specifically, the invention of "smart objects" as for the Internet of Things (IoT)—that is, groups of physical objects that are embedded with sensors and software processing ability to exchange large amounts of data with other devices over the Internet or other communications networks (see, for a review, Sestino et al., 2020)—is poised to radically transform physical stores and consumers' buying into an integrated and interactive shopping experience (Pantano & Dennis, 2019).

This technological integration was made possible both through the online presence of companies, available by means of social networks, e-commerce platforms (Siddiqui et al., 2003), and the pervasive integration of new technologies within stores (Grewal et al., 2017). This is the case of the IoT that may support in-store customers during their shopping experience (Grewal et al., 2020; Kim et al., 2017). Consequently, marketing managers' efforts are now no longer limited to a simple online presence through e-commerce sites, social media, or blogs (Okonkwo, 2009). By integrating various digital tools into physical distribution spaces (e.g., touch screens, interactive totems, Wi-Fi connectivity, Voice Assistants and, generally, smart objects), they may deeply enrich end consumers' experiences (Amatulli et al., 2022; Lawry & Choi, 2013), with positive impacts of consumers' perception of their brands too. Such changes are already impacting consumers' perceptions of many brands for the better (Amatulli et al., 2021; Sestino et al., 2021a).

In the fashion sector, the integration of these new technologies has revitalized the firms' supply chain (Braglia et al., 2020). In particular, blockchain technologies (Azzi et al., 2019) have opened new opportunities for certifying and tracking the origin and the production path of products sent to final markets (Saberi et al., 2019). Likewise, applications based on blockchain technologies, such as NFTs (Gorkhali et al., 2020), represent an opportunity to offer fashion customers unique products and richer shopping experiences.

Granted, individual characteristics may play a fundamental role in shaping consumers' willingness to use such technologies and, by extension, their intention to buy proposed fashion products (Amatulli et al., 2021;

Park et al., 2020). Amidst the introduction of new technologies, *consumers' innovativeness* may come to play a central role by interacting with their status consumption orientation. Consumers' innovativeness is defined as their propensity to accept change and desire to be among the first to try or buy new products (Hoffman et al., 2010; Park et al., 2010; Wanberg & Banas, 2000). This is particularly relevant for those consumers who buy fashion products for hedonic purposes, as they are typically characterized by a strong status consumption orientation (O'Cass & McEwen, 2004).

Based on these premises, this study explores the interplay of these two consumers' characteristics—that is, innovativeness and status consumption orientation—in determining their intention to purchase fashion products which incorporate a high level of technology and, more specifically, NFT-based fashion products.

2   THEORETICAL BACKGROUND

Technological innovations can improve consumers' experiences flowing from products and services to the point of becoming integral part of them. In this scenario, NFTs' technologies are already being incorporated into fashion products in order to enhance collections and increase shoppers' engagement (Business of Fashion, 2021; Raman & Benson, 2021).

The fashion industry's first NFT experiment occurred—as mentioned in a previous chapter—in the sneakers market, where RTFKT Studios proposed their own branded pair of virtual sneakers. The Studios launched a collaboration with the designer Fewocious, who specializes in digital art, for creating a limited collection of 600 NFT-based sneakers accompanied by two different capsules of merchandising (Nssmag, 2021). Shoppers had the chance to try on the sneakers via augmented reality on the social network "Snapchat" and the opportunity to get a physical copy. However, as the designer highlighted, the real value was in the digital versions of the products, which were certified as unique and authentic, and could subsequently be shown off in virtual spaces.

This example embodies how NFTs' diffusion can renew the concept of "exclusivity" (Wang et al., 2021) in design and fashion markets. Indeed, as the NFTs' definition suggests ("Non-Fungible" means "non-replaceable"), an NFT is a unique digital element that represents only the object it is associated with (Ante, 2021): Its uniqueness is protected by the blockchain tracking system and, therefore, each NFT represents the sole artifact of its kind. Even if as digital files NFTs can be reproduced and copied, the "signature" of an NFT always makes it recognizable the original artifact and, consequently, a single and "registered" author who created such a digital product.

Even luxury brands' companies, which are typically slow adopters, are beginning to appreciate this technology: Gucci launched a version of virtual sneakers, called "Gucci Virtual 22," in March 2021 (The Guardian, 2021). Purchasers could virtually show off and share the sneakers with their followers on major social networks (mainly Instagram, Snapchat) or in the virtual world (such as Decentraland). As a result of a collaboration between Gucci and the fashion-tech company Wanna, such digital shoes were available for purchase through the mobile apps of both Gucci and Wanna. Other companies followed suit: The DressX mobile application (www.dressx.com), for instance, allowed one to wear virtual clothes and participate in real virtual fashion shows (DressX, 2021). This trend has also spread to gaming platforms, as in the case of the abovementioned collaboration between the League of Legends and Louis Vuitton (Vogue, 2021). When the game's world championships were held in Paris in 2019, the Louis Vuitton Maison created a clothing line that players could buy and equip on their "in-game" characters. Naturally, all such digital products were sold as NFTs to signal one's ownership of a unique good and, by extension, one's status.

Due to the novelty of this technology, *consumers' innovativeness* could positively influence their intention to purchase such products. Indeed, some may desire to be among the first in the market to possess these technology-based fashion products (Amatulli et al., 2014; Hoffman et al., 2010; Steenkamp & Gielens, 2003). Coherently, past studies have shown that fashion consumers characterized by a high level of innovativeness are constantly looking for novelty and variety in fashion collections (Workman & Johnson, 1993). Because consumers' innovativeness may enhance the actual adoption of new products, marketers could leverage this orientation through properly designed salient advertising and communication strategies (Guido, 2001; Hirunyawipada & Paswan, 2006). Based on the foregoing, we hypothesized the following:

Hp 1: Consumers' innovativeness is positively related to their intention to purchase NFT-based fashion products.

The literature has highlighted that innovative fashion consumers—in comparison to their less innovative counterparts—seem more comfortable, pleasant, contemporary, formal, colorful, and particularly vain

(Goldsmith et al., 1999). These traits often reflect consumers' "desires to gain prestige from the acquisition of status-laden products and brands" (O'Cass & McEwen, 2004, p. 27). That said, little is known about the role of status consumption in the field of fashion digital products, and the few investigations conducted so far have provided inconclusive results. For instance, the study presented in Chap. 5 (above) revealed a positive, but only marginally significant, effect of status consumption orientation on consumers' intention to purchase NFT-based music compilations.

Therefore, it is possible that the influence of status consumption orientation on consumers' intention to buy these new digital products could be moderated by individual variables such as consumers' level of innovativeness. Essentially, while consumers with stronger status consumption orientation tend to be attracted by advertising messages that promote a product's ability to positively impact their status (Eastman et al., 1999; Sestino et al., 2021), it is feasible that this tendency has no effect on their intention to purchase NFT-based fashion products unless such consumers are innovative enough to appreciate these hyper-technological products. Therefore, in addition to serving as a direct antecedent of consumers' intention to purchase NFT-based fashion products, we expect that consumers' innovativeness also moderates the relationship between status consumption orientation and such consumers' intention (see Fig. 6.1). More specifically, we further hypothesized the following:

Hp 2: Consumers' innovativeness moderates the relationship between status consumption orientation and consumers' intention to purchase NFT-based fashion products in such a way that this relationship is positive and significant only for consumers with higher levels of innovativeness.

3 Methodology

To test our two hypotheses, we conducted a survey study by administering a structured questionnaire to a sample of 182 international respondents, who were recruited online via Amazon's Mechanical Turk. Subjects were asked to indicate their level of innovativeness, by using eight items adapted from previous studies (Bruner, 2013; Steenkamp & Gielens, 2003)—that is, "When I see a new product on the shelf, I would like to give it a try," "In general, I am among the first to buy new products when they appear

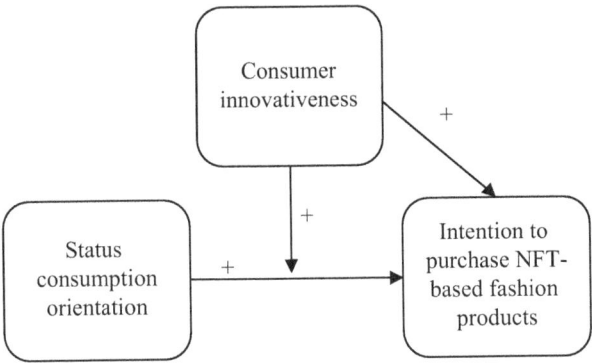

Fig. 6.1 The influence of consumer innovativeness and status consumption orientation on consumers' intention to purchase NFT-based fashion products

on the market," "If I like a brand, I could switch from it just to try something new," "I am very curious in trying new and different products," "I am usually among the first to try new brands," "Sometimes I buy new brands about which I am uncertain how they will perform," "I enjoy taking chances in buying new products," and "I like to buy a new product before other people do." They were also asked to indicate their level of status consumption orientation, by using five items adapted from Eastman et al. (1999) (e.g., "I would buy a product just because it has status"), as in the previous study. Responses on these two sets of items were rated on seven-point Likert scales (1 = "Strongly disagree," 7 = "Strongly agree").

In the second part of the questionnaire, subjects were presented with a scenario in which they saw an ad message regarding the use of NFTs in the fashion market. More specifically, they read about a pair of NFT-based sneakers they could virtually wear, through their avatar in the Metaverse, and that the NFTs' technology would have assured uniqueness, authenticity, and exclusivity. Following that, respondents indicated their intention to purchase such virtual shoes by using the usual three items adapted from Dodds et al. (1991)—for example, "I would buy that pair of sneakers" (see the previous chapter)—and assessed on a seven-point Likert scale (1 = "Strongly disagree", 7 = "Strongly agree"). Finally, they provided sociodemographic data regarding their age, gender, education level, and nationality.

4 RESULTS

4.1 Sample Description

The sample comprised 182 respondents with an average age of 46.38 years (SD = 11.07); 66.5% of them were men and 33.5% were women. Regarding their education level, 27.5% held a high-school diploma, 67% held a bachelor's or master's degree, and 5.5% held a doctoral degree. Most respondents lived in Europe (31.9%) and India (31.3%); the others lived in the United States (14.3%), China (13.2%), and Canada (9.3%).

4.2 Descriptive and Reliability Statistics

Multi-item scales measuring consumers' innovativeness, status consumption orientation, and intention to purchase were checked for internal consistency. To this end, we computed a Cronbach's alpha index for each of these constructs. The three obtained alpha coefficients were adequately high (*consumer innovativeness*: α = 0.92; *status consumption orientation*: α = 0.92; *purchase intention*: α = 0.93). Therefore, for each of the three multi-item scales, we averaged the scores obtained on each of the respective items to constitute an aggregate measure of the corresponding construct (*consumer innovativeness*: M = 4.93, SD = 1.32; *status consumption orientation*: M = 3.95, SD = 1.80; *purchase intention*: M = 5.64, SD = 1.12).

4.3 Hypothesis Testing

To test our hypotheses, we estimated a moderated regression model by using the SPSS PROCESS macro (Model 1) developed by Hayes (2022). The model expressed consumers' intention to purchase the NFT-based sneakers as a function of their innovativeness (treated as a continuous, mean-centered variable), status consumption orientation (as a continuous, mean-centered variable), and their interaction, while statistically controlling for their age, gender (coded as a binary variable taking the value 1 = female and 0 = male), and education level (1 = high-school diploma, 2 = bachelor's or master's degree, 3 = doctoral degree).

Potential multicollinearity among the independent variables employed in the moderated regression model was excluded as variance inflation factor coefficients were lower than 2, thus below the recommended threshold of 10 (Hair et al., 2013).

Table 6.1 Results of the moderated regression analysis showing the interplay of consumer innovativeness and status consumption orientation in determining the purchase intention of NFT-based fashion products

Independent Variable	b	SE	t	p
Constant	4.34	0.47	9.24	< 0.001
Age	0.01	0.01	1.93	0.055
Gender	0.17	0.16	1.04	0.301
Education level	0.26	0.14	1.82	0.070
Status consumption orientation (X)	0.03	0.06	0.54	0.590
Consumer innovativeness (W)	0.33	0.08	4.31	< 0.001
Interaction term ($X \times W$)	0.09	0.03	2.92	0.004
Effect of X on the dependent variable conditional to the level of W				
	b	SE	t	p
Low level of W ($M - 1SD$)	−0.09	0.07	−1.19	0.237
High level of W ($M + 1SD$)	0.15	0.06	2.37	0.019

Note: $N = 182$. Dependent variable: Intention to purchase the advertised sneakers. Gender coded as 1 = female and 0 = male. Education level coded as 1 = high-school diploma, 2 = bachelor's or master's degree, 3 = doctoral degree. Fit statistics: $R = 0.50$, $R^2 = 0.25$, Std. error of the estimate = 0.97, $F(6, 175) = 9.92$, $p < 0.001$

Consistent with *Hp 1*, the obtained results, summarized in Table 6.1, revealed a significant positive relationship between consumers' level of innovativeness and their intention to purchase the advertised sneakers ($b = 0.33$, $p < 0.001$). Conversely, the relationship between status consumption orientation and purchase intention was non-significant ($p = 0.590$). More importantly, the results showed a significant effect of the interaction term (*status consumption orientation × consumer innovativeness*) on the purchase intention that was positive and significant ($b = 0.09$, $p = 0.004$). We delved deeper into the nature of this interaction by estimating the effect of status consumption orientation on the purchase intention at lower ($M - 1SD$) and higher ($M + 1SD$) levels of innovativeness. In line with *Hp 2*, the obtained results showed that the effect of status consumption orientation was non-significant for respondents with a lower level of innovativeness ($p = 0.237$), whereas it was positive and significant for respondents with a higher level of innovativeness ($b = 0.15$, $p = 0.019$).

Figure 6.2 displays how consumers' purchase intention varies as a function of their levels of innovativeness and status consumption orientation.

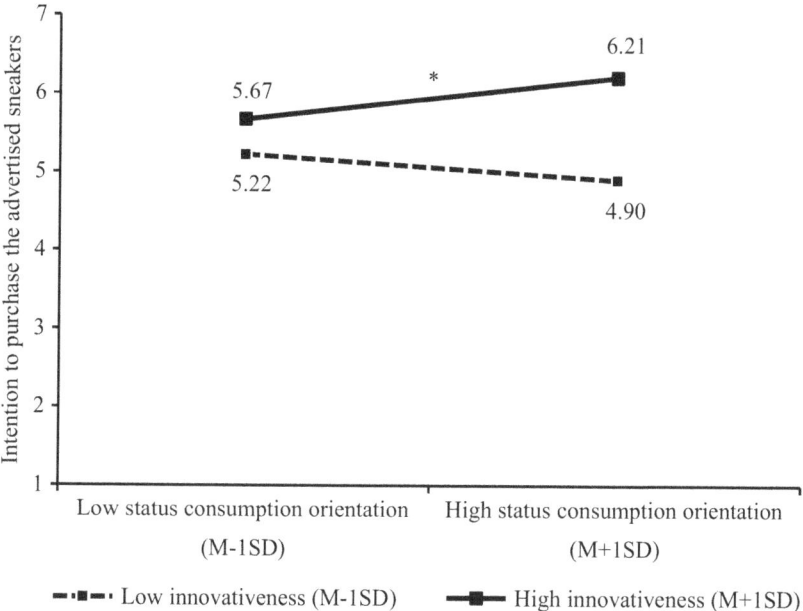

Fig. 6.2 Purchase intention of NFT-based fashion products as a function of consumer innovativeness and status consumption orientation. (*Note: * Conditional effect significant at a 0.05 level*)

5 DISCUSSION AND IMPLICATIONS

The rapid surge in interest around NFTs may have interesting implications in the fashion market not only in terms of certifying and reselling physical garments but also with regard to spreading digital fashion (Wang et al., 2021).

Being able to wear a favorite clothing in a virtual world, without actually dressing that object physically, is now a possibility (Chohan & Paschen, 2021). That said, the effects of NFTs' technologies on consumers' intention to buy such products and the role of individuals' characteristics in determining this intention are still hazy. Our study contributed to fill this gap by exploring the roles of two important consumers' characteristics: consumers' innovativeness and their status consumption orientation. More specifically, our study investigated the interplay of consumer innovativeness and status consumption orientation in determining consumers' intention to purchase NFT-based fashion products.

The obtained results revealed that consumers' innovativeness positively influences their intention to buy certain NFT-based fashion products (i.e., digital sneakers). Furthermore, status consumption orientation contributes to determining purchase intention especially for individuals with higher levels of innovativeness. This essentially means that NFT-based digital products tend to be purchased for hedonic purposes and, more particularly, for their ability to signal prestige and status to others especially when consumers are innovative and, as such, seek to be among the first in their social circles to possess such hyper-technological goods.

Theoretically, our findings contribute to the literature on fashion product consumption by demonstrating that consumers' innovativeness could play a relevant role in the consumption of new fashion products available in the Metaverse—that is, where individuals are represented by three-dimensional avatars (Kim, 2021; Stephenson, 2003). Furthermore, such a form of digital possession could play a status-signaling function and, thus, be pursued as a way to show off among innovative consumers.

Managerially, our findings suggest that fashion marketing managers, together with stylists and designers, can leverage such technologies to improve consumers' experiences and communicate their offerings. To succeed in this emerging market, they should primarily target NFT-based offerings at innovative consumers, in order to get them to buy such offerings out of a synergic effect of their level innovativeness and status consumption orientation.

Future studies might expand our evidence by considering other variables, such as price perception, cognitive involvement, emotional engagement, arousal, and other affective states potentially associated with new virtual shopping and consumption experiences.

REFERENCES

Amatulli, C., De Angelis, M., Sestino, A., & Guido, G. (2021). Omnichannel Shopping Experiences for Fast Fashion and Luxury Brands: An Exploratory Study. In F. Mosca, C. Casalegno, & R. Gallo (Eds.), *Developing Successful Global Strategies for Marketing Luxury Brands* (pp. 22–43). New York, NY.

Amatulli, C., Guido, G., & Barbarito, C. M. (2014). Does Popularity in Social Networks Influence Purchasing and Lifestyle Decisions? The Meaning of Online Friendship. *Journal of Media Business Studies, 11*(3), 1–21.

Amatulli, C., Sestino, A., Peluso, A. M., & Guido, G. (2022). Luxury Hospitality and the Adoption of Voice Assistants: The Role of Openness to Change and

Status Consumption. In A. S. Kotur & S. K. Dixit (Eds.), *The Emerald Handbook of Luxury Management for Hospitality and Tourism* (pp. 285–303). Emerald Publishing Limited.

Ante, L. (2021). The Non-Fungible Token (NFT) Market and its Relationship with Bitcoin and Ethereum. BRL Working Paper Series, No. 20.

Azzi, R., Chamoun, R. K., & Sokhn, M. (2019). The Power of a Blockchain-Based Supply Chain. *Computers & Industrial Engineering, 135*(1), 582–592.

Balaji, M. S., & Roy, S. K. (2017). Value Co-Creation with Internet of Things Technology in the Retail Industry. *Journal of Marketing Management, 33*(1-2), 7–31.

Braglia, M., Marrazzini, L., Padellini, L., & Rinaldi, R. (2020). Managerial and Industry 4.0 Solutions for Fashion Supply Chains. Journal of Fashion Marketing and Management: An. *International Journal, 25*(1), 184–201.

Bruner, G. C. (2013). *Marketing Scales Handbook: Multi-Item Measures for Consumer Insight Research* (Vol. 7). GCBII Productions.

Business of Fashion. (2021). The State of Fashion 2021 Report: Finding Promise in Perilous Times. Retrieved January 8, 2022, from https://www.businessof-fashion.com/reports/news-analysis/the-state-of-fashion-2021-industry-report-bof-mckinsey/

Chohan, R., & Paschen, J. (2021, in press). *What Marketers Need to Know about Non-Fungible Tokens (NFTs)*. Business Horizons.

Dodds, W. B., Monroe, K. B., & Grewal, D. (1991). Effects of Price, Brand, and Store Information on Buyers' Product Evaluations. *Journal of Marketing Research, 28*(3), 307–319.

DressX. (2021). DressX Official. Retrieved January 15, 2022, from https://dressx.com

Eastman, J. K., Goldsmith, R. E., & Flynn, L. R. (1999). Status Consumption in Consumer Behavior: Scale Development and Validation. *Journal of Marketing Theory and Practice, 7*(3), 41–52.

Goldsmith, R. E., Moore, M. A., & Beaudoin, P. (1999). Fashion Innovativeness and Self-Concept: A Replication. *Journal of Product & Brand Management, 8*(1), 7–18.

Gorkhali, A., Li, L., & Shrestha, A. (2020). Blockchain: A Literature Review. *Journal of Management Analytics, 7*(3), 321–343.

Grewal, D., Noble, S. M., Roggeveen, A. L., & Nordfalt, J. (2020). The Future of In-store Technology. *Journal of the Academy of Marketing Science, 48*(1), 96–113.

Grewal, D., Roggeveen, A. L., & Nordfält, J. (2017). The Future of Retailing. *Journal of Retailing, 93*(1), 1–6.

Guido, G. (2001). *The Salience of Marketing Stimuli: An Incongruity-Salience Hypothesis on Consumer Awareness*. Kluwer Academic Publishers.

Hair, J. F., Black, W. C., Babin, B. J., & Anderson, R. E. (2013). *Multivariate Data Analysis*. Pearson.

Hayes, A. F. (2022). *Introduction to Mediation, Moderation, and Conditional Process Analysis: A Regression-Based Approach*. The Guilford Press.

Hirunyawipada, T., & Paswan, A. K. (2006). Consumer Innovativeness and Perceived Risk: Implications for High Technology Product Adoption. *Journal of Consumer Marketing, 23*(4), 182–198.

Hoffman, D. L., Kopalle, P. K., & Novak, T. P. (2010). The "Right" Consumers for Better Concepts: Identifying Consumers High in Emergent Nature to Develop New Product Concepts. *Journal of Marketing Research, 47*(5), 854–865.

Hoyer, W. D., Kroschke, M., Schmitt, B., Kraume, K., & Shankar, V. (2020). Transforming the Customer Experience through New Technologies. *Journal of Interactive Marketing, 51*(1), 57–71.

Kim, H. Y., Lee, J. Y., Mun, J. M., & Johnson, K. K. (2017). Consumer Adoption of Smart In-Store Technology: Assessing the Predictive Value of Attitude Versus Beliefs in the Technology Acceptance Model. *International Journal of Fashion Design, Technology and Education, 10*(1), 26–36.

Kim, J. (2021). Advertising in the Metaverse: Research Agenda. *Journal of Interactive Advertising, 21*(3), 141–144.

Lawry, C. A., & Choi, L. (2013). The Omnichannel Luxury Retail Experience: Building Mobile Trust and Technology Acceptance of Quick Response (QR) Codes. *Marketing ZFP, 35*(2), 144–154.

Lynch, S., & Barnes, L. (2020). Omnichannel Fashion Retailing: Examining the Customer Decision-Making Journey. *Journal of Fashion Marketing and Management: An International Journal, 24*(3), 471–493.

Nssmag. (2021). A Study of Fashion Brand Perception 2021. Retrieved January 12, 2022, from https://data.nssmag.com/docs/CARTESIO

O'Cass, A., & McEwen, H. (2004). Exploring Consumer Status and Conspicuous Consumption. *Journal of Consumer Behaviour, 4*(1), 25–39.

Okonkwo, U. (2009). Sustaining the Luxury Brand on the Internet. *Journal of Brand Management, 16*(5), 302–310.

Pantano, E., & Dennis, C. (2019). Store Buildings as Tourist Attractions: Mining Retail Meaning of Store Building Pictures Through a Machine Learning Approach. *Journal of Retailing and Consumer Services, 51*, 304–310.

Park, J. E., Yu, J., & Zhou, J. X. (2010). Consumer Innovativeness and Shopping Styles. *Journal of Consumer Marketing, 27*(5), 437–446.

Park, J. S., Ha, S., & Jeong, S. W. (2020). Consumer Acceptance of Self-Service Technologies in Fashion Retail Stores. *Journal of Fashion Marketing and Management: An International Journal, 25*(2), 372–388.

Raman, R., & Benson, E. R. (2021). The World of NFTs (Non-Fungible Tokens): The Future of Blockchain and Asset Ownership. In B. M. Adel & L. Chaari

Fourati (Eds.), *Enabling Blockchain Technology for Secure Networking and Communications* (pp. 89–108). IGI Global.

Saberi, S., Kouhizadeh, M., Sarkis, J., & Shen, L. (2019). Blockchain Technology and Its Relationships to Sustainable Supply Chain Management. *International Journal of Production Research, 57*(7), 2117–2135.

Sestino, A., Amatulli, C., & De Angelis, M. (2021a, in press). Retail e Nuove Tecnologie nel Fashion: Effetti su Shopping Experience e Brand "Luxuryfication". Micro & Macro Marketing. https://www.rivisteweb.it/doi/10.1431/103223

Sestino, A., Prete, M. I., Piper, L., & Guido, G. (2020). Internet of Things and Big Data as Enablers for Business Digitalization Strategies. *Technovation, 98*(C), 102173–102181.

Sestino, A., Prete, M. I., Piper, L., & Guido, G. (2021). The Future of Online Marketing Strategies and Digital Tools: New Challenges and Contribution to the RACE Framework. *International Journal of Electronic Trade.* https://doi.org/10.1504/IJETRADE.2021.10042594

Siddiqui, N., O'Malley, A., McColl, J. C., & Birtwistle, G. (2003). Retailer and Consumer Perceptions of Online Fashion Retailers: Web Site Design Issues. *Journal of Fashion Marketing and Management: An International Journal, 7*(4), 345–355.

Steenkamp, J. B. E., & Gielens, K. (2003). Consumer and Market Drivers of the Trial Probability of New Consumer Packaged Goods. *Journal of Consumer Research, 30*(3), 368–384.

Stephenson, N. (2003). *Snow Crash: A Novel.* Spectra.

The Guardian. (2021). A Virtual Steal: The Digital Gucci Sneakers for Sale at $17.99. Retrieved November 11, 2021, from https://www.theguardian.com/fashion/2021/mar/19/a-virtual-steal-the-gucci-sneakers-for-sale-at-1799

Vogue. (2021). Dolce & Gabbana Porta gli NFT nel Mondo della Moda. Retrieved December 30, 2022, from https://www.vogue.it/moda/article/dolce-gabbana-ntf-haute-couture-moda-venezia

Wanberg, C. R., & Banas, J. T. (2000). Predictors and Outcomes of Openness to Changes in a Reorganizing Workplace. *Journal of Applied Psychology, 85*(1), 132.

Wang, Q., Li, R., Wang, Q., & Chen, S. (2021). Non-Fungible Token (NFT): Overview, Evaluation, Opportunities and Challenges. Retrieved December 1, 2021, from https://arxiv.org/abs/2105.07447

Workman, J. E., & Johnson, K. K. (1993). Fashion Opinion Leadership, Fashion Innovativeness, and Need for Variety. *Clothing and Textiles Research Journal, 11*(3), 60–64.

CHAPTER 7

Conclusions

Abstract This chapter concludes the book with *further reflections* on the marketing relevance of NFTs for consumers' perception of their extended selves, a summary of the results obtained in the three empirical studies presented in Chaps. 4, 5, and 6, and a discussion of their *theoretical and marketing implications* along with major limitations and future research directions.

Keywords NFTs • Materialism • Consumer innovativeness • Status consumption orientation • Theoretical and marketing implications • Future research

1 WHEN CONSUMPTION GOES BEYOND MATERIAL POSSESSIONS

Nowadays, digital technologies are integral to the growth of businesses and societies—hence the mounting efforts to offer renewed products and restructured services to consumers. Crises like the COVID-19 pandemic (still ongoing when this book was written) have accelerated the development and diffusion of these new technologies (e.g., blockchain, IoT, AI, VR, Big Data). Thus, consumers face a "new normalcy" (Amatulli et al., 2021) characterized by the pervasive use of technological tools, where digital and physical spaces overlap and interact.

A. Sestino et al., *Non-Fungible Tokens (NFTs)*,
https://doi.org/10.1007/978-3-031-07203-1_7

Against this backdrop, blockchain applications present new opportunities to activate "digital tools" that are used in the virtual world and possessed in real-life: Non-Fungible Tokens (NFTs). Using the blockchain, NFTs can permanently certify the ownership of a virtual object by recording information to a distributed ledger (Chohan & Paschen, 2021; Sestino et al., 2022). In this way, NFTs permit the transfer of the ownership rights regarding digital objects—such as a weapon in a video game, a fashion accessory that can be worn around a virtual world, a specific music file, and so on. The safe and transparent nature of data storage on the blockchain can have major implications for marketing studies, especially in terms of advertising strategies that promote digital products.

Importantly, the literature shows that consumers' behaviors and purchase intentions are led by the sense of material possession that the desired object may confer (Belk, 1985). Seminal studies (i.e., Belk, 1988) have demonstrated that consumers' possessions are "the major contributor to and reflection of individuals' identities" (p. 139) and involves consumer behavior rather than buyer behavior, appearing to be a much richer construct than previous formulations positing a relationship between self-concept and consumer brand choice. Coherently, the concept of consumers' materialism reflects the importance they attribute to worldly possessions (Amatulli & Guido, 2012; Belk, 2013). Sometimes, extensive possessions become the only instrument by which materialistic consumers can increase their personal satisfaction and societal standing.

Belk (1984) observed three main characteristics regarding material possessions: first, possessiveness, whereby consumers tend to buy goods in order to retain control or ownership of them; second, non-generosity, whereby consumers are unwilling to give or share their possessions with others; and third, envy, whereby consumers express displeasure toward other individuals who have more goods. However, in the modern world, possessiveness often seems the most important trait driving consumers' behaviors and purchase intentions (Ger, 2005; Veer & Shankar, 2011). Sometimes, possessiveness also serves as a conduit to displaying one's status (Richins, 2004).

In our deeply technological society, the issue of possessiveness may contain interesting opportunities for marketers and managers. Indeed, a few past studies (e.g., Denegri-Knott & Molesworth, 2013; Fritze et al., 2019; Watkins et al., 2016) have shown that consumers' desire to form meaningful attachments to possessions may extend to the immaterial digital world:

We can see this behavior, for example, in videogames where people create personal avatars or collect virtual objects (Watkins et al., 2016). However, research has yet to explore how consumers may come to use (and even prefer) new digital instruments, such as NFTs, in order to satisfy their yearning for materialism, status, and innovativeness.

2   IN SUMMARY

This book explored how consumers' individual differences might shape the effectiveness of NFT-oriented marketing strategies. Specifically, our preliminary findings suggest that marketing managers should mold their digital offerings around consumers' desire for unicity, prestige, and exclusivity, as expressed by their materialism, status consumption orientation, and innovativeness in relation to certain items (e.g., artworks, music files, fashion products). These individual traits may provide a useful metric for segmenting the market and designing suitable advertising stimuli. Furthermore, we presented the most current depiction of the marketing literature in relation to the current issues and uses of NFT-based business offers. Specifically, we outlined new opportunities in the world of intellectual property (e.g., digital art, academia, memes and viral contents), lifestyles (sport & leisure, fashion, virtual worlds), and entertainment (music & movies, games, and other products).

Finally, in Chaps. 4, 5, and 6, we investigated some specific consumer variables and their influence on the intention to purchase NFT-based products. Three studies, respectively, covered them in art, music, and fashion settings.

Chapter 4 acknowledged that NFTs have the potential to revolutionize the art context thanks to the newfound possibility of uniquely owning a digital artwork. This chapter emphasized that individuals who buy such an artwork do not simply appreciate its cultural value, but also seek to satisfy a desire for material possessions. It presented a survey study on the influence of *materialism* on consumers' intention to purchase NFT-based works of art. Our findings shed light on the role of materialism by showing the relevance of this individual characteristic to determining consumers' intention to buy NFT-based artworks, especially in communication contexts that emphasize the benefits of unicity and exclusive ownership deriving from NFTs' technology. Thus, based on our results, marketing managers of digital artworks should lean on consumers' materialism when segmenting their target markets.

Chapter 5 considered the music market, where consumers who are passionate about the subject often develop affectionate relationships with objects that help them feel connected to their favorite artists (CDs, vinyl records, and so on). However, there is an open question as to how consumers will relate to NFTs (which are immaterial by nature) in this domain (Krohn-Grimberghe, 2020; Magaudda, 2011). This chapter presented a survey study on the effect of *status consumption orientation*—in addition to materialism—on consumers' intention to purchase some NFT-based music compilation. Our findings were in line with those presented previously; however, they provide initial evidence for a determining the role of status consumption orientation insofar as this consumer characteristic is able to affect consumers' intention to buy such products.

Chapter 6 focused on the fashion market: A field that is beginning to leverage NFTs in order to enrich consumers' shopping experiences. When promoting NFT-based products, fashion managers can rely on the baseline benefits of the blockchain technology (Patrickson, 2021), but they also need to know the characteristics that drive fashion consumers to buy and use these new products which can be worn in the virtual world. The chapter presented a survey study on the synergic role of *consumer innovativeness* and *status consumption orientation* in determining consumers' intention to purchase NFT-based fashion products. Our findings showed a positive influence of consumers' innovativeness on their purchase intention. Furthermore, they clarified the role of status consumption orientation, which appeared only marginally significant in the previous study. More specifically, our findings suggested a triggering role for consumer innovativeness, whereby status consumption orientation exerts a positive influence on consumers' intention *only* in the presence of a high (as compared to a low) level of innovativeness. This implies that, for innovative consumers, buying an NFT-based fashion product—such as a pair of virtual sneakers—may be a new way to show off and signal their own status to their others.

It is worth noting that the results of our three empirical studies emerged within research settings where respondents saw ad messages that emphasized the unique characteristics of NFTs in terms of uniqueness, authenticity, and exclusive ownership. Therefore, marketing managers of NFT-based products interested in leveraging our findings in their segmentation, targeting, and communication strategies should appropriately emphasize such characteristics. Taken together, the results of our three empirical studies provide preliminary but valuable insights for marketing managers who want to understand the best ways to communicate the benefits of NFTs.

It appears that consumers' *materialism, status consumption orientation,* and *innovativeness* can play a role in the digital world that is as relevant as the one they typically play in the real world. In relation to NFTs, marketing campaigns should strive to leverage these digital tools to satisfy consumers' materialistic urges as well as their desires to express status and to be among the first in their social circles to own such hyper-technological products. Put differently: Before investing in NFT advertising, firms should try to understand the extent to which their customers seek material possessions, are motivated to signal their status to others, and be among the first purchasers of NFT-based products, thus projecting their extended self-perception in the digital environment.

To close, our research features several limitations. Among the main ones, our studies have focused on a relatively small set of psychological antecedents (i.e., materialism, status consumption orientation, innovativeness) and did not consider other potentially relevant predictors. Thus, future studies could profitably investigate other product-related characteristics (e.g., perceived usefulness, ease of use), company- and/or market-related characteristics (e.g., corporate reputation, market concentration), as well as contextual factors (e.g., the presence of other owners of NFTs in the surrounding).

Humanity's movement into this new digital landscape represents a fertile ground for research; now is the time for scholars to begin planting seeds and assessing the possibilities of the unknown.

REFERENCES

Amatulli, C., De Angelis, M., Sestino, A., & Guido, G. (2021). Omnichannel Shopping Experiences for Fast Fashion and Luxury Brands: An Exploratory Study. In F. Mosca, C. Casalegno, & R. Gallo (Eds.), *Developing Successful Global Strategies for Marketing Luxury Brands* (pp. 22–43). New York, NY.
Amatulli, C., & Guido, G. (2012). Externalized vs. Internalized Consumption of Luxury Goods: Propositions and Implications for Luxury Retail Marketing. *The International Review of Retail, Distribution and Consumer Research, 22*(2), 189–207.

Belk, R. W. (1984). Three Scales to Measure Constructs Related to Materialism: Reliability, Validity, and Relationships to Measures of Happiness. *Advances in Consumer Research, 11*(1), 291–297.

Belk, R. W. (1985). Materialism: Trait Aspects of Living in the Material World. *Journal of Consumer Research, 12*(3), 265–280.

Belk, R. W. (1988). Possessions and the Extended Self. *Journal of Consumer Research, 15*(2), 139–168.

Belk, R. W. (2013). Extended Self in a Digital World. *Journal of Consumer Research, 40*(3), 477–500.

Chohan, R., & Paschen, J. (2021, in press). *What Marketers Need to Know about Non-Fungible Tokens (NFTs)*. Business Horizons.

Denegri-Knott, J., & Molesworth, M. (2013). Redistributed Consumer Desire in Digital Virtual Worlds of Consumption. *Journal of Marketing Management, 29*(13-14), 1561–1579.

Fritze, M. P., Eisingerich, A. B., & Benkenstein, M. (2019). Digital Transformation and Possession Attachment: Examining the Endowment Effect for Consumers' Relationships with Hedonic and Utilitarian Digital Service Technologies. *Electronic Commerce Research, 19*(2), 311–337.

Ger, G. (2005). Special Session Summary Religion and Consumption: The Profane Sacred. *Advances in Consumer Research, 32*(1), 79–81.

Krohn-Grimberghe, L. (2020). The Dematerialization of Music: How Streaming Technology Impacts Music Production and Consumption. In M. Trondle (Ed.), *Classical Concert Studies* (pp. 296–308). Routledge.

Magaudda, P. (2011). When Materiality 'Bites Back': Digital Music Consumption Practices in the Age of Dematerialization. *Journal of Consumer Culture, 11*(1), 15–36.

Patrickson, B. (2021). What do Blockchain Technologies Imply for Digital Creative Industries? *Creativity and Innovation Management, 30*(3), 585–595.

Richins, M. L. (2004). The Material Values Scale: Measurement Properties and Development of a Short Form. *Journal of Consumer Research, 31*(1), 209–219.

Sestino, A., Giraldi, L., Cedrola, E., & Guido, G. (2022). The Relevance of Individuals' Perceived Data Protection Level on Intention to Use Blockchain-Based Mobile Apps. An Experimental Study. In M. Al-Emran (Ed.), *Recent Innovations in Artificial Intelligence and Smart Applications*. Springer International Publishing, in press.

Veer, E., & Shankar, A. (2011). Forgive Me, Father, for I Did Not Give Full Justification for My Sins: How Religious Consumers Justify the Acquisition of Material Wealth. *Journal of Marketing Management, 27*(5-6), 547–560.

Watkins, R. D., Denegri-Knott, J., & Molesworth, M. (2016). The Relationship Between Ownership and Possession: Observations from the Context of Digital Virtual Goods. *Journal of Marketing Management, 32*(1-2), 44–70.

REFERENCES

Agenda Digitale. (2022). NFT and Intellectual Property: This Is How the Blockchain Supports the Protection of Rights. Retrieved March 8, 2022, from https://www.agendadigitale.eu/documenti/nft-e-proprieta-intellettuale-ecco-come-la-blockchain-supporta-la-tutela-dei-diritti

AGI. (2021). Che C'Entra la Blockchain con Picasso: A Cosa Servono gli NFT. Retrieved December 12, 2021, from https://www.agi.it/economia/news/2021-03-26/cosa-sono-nft-a-cosa-servono-11920239/

Aguinis, H., Villamor, I., & Ramani, R. S. (2021). MTurk Research: Review and Recommendations. *Journal of Management, 47*(4), 823–837.

Ahmad, N., & Abdulkarim, H. (2019). The Impact of Flow Experience and Personality Type on the Intention to Use Virtual World. *International Journal of Human–Computer Interaction, 35*(12), 1074–1085.

Amatulli, C., De Angelis, M., Sestino, A., & Guido, G. (2021). Omnichannel Shopping Experiences for Fast Fashion and Luxury Brands: An Exploratory Study. In F. Mosca, C. Casalegno, & R. Gallo (Eds.), *Developing Successful Global Strategies for Marketing Luxury Brands* (pp. 22–43). New York, NY.

Amatulli, C., & Guido, G. (2011). Determinants of Purchasing Intention for Fashion Luxury Goods in the Italian Market: A Laddering Approach. *Journal of Fashion Marketing and Management, 15*(1), 123–136.

Amatulli, C., & Guido, G. (2012). Externalized vs. Internalized Consumption of Luxury Goods: Propositions and Implications for Luxury Retail Marketing. *The International Review of Retail, Distribution and Consumer Research, 22*(2), 189–207.

Amatulli, C., Guido, G., & Barbarito, C. M. (2014). Does Popularity in Social Networks Influence Purchasing and Lifestyle Decisions? The Meaning of Online Friendship. *Journal of Media Business Studies, 11*(3), 1–21.

Amatulli, C., Peluso, A. M., Guido, G., & Yoon, C. (2018). When Feeling Younger Depends on Others: The Effects of Social Cues on Older Consumers. *Journal of Consumer Research, 45*(4), 691–709.

Amatulli, C., Sestino, A., Peluso, A. M., & Guido, G. (2022). Luxury Hospitality and the Adoption of Voice Assistants: The Role of Openness to Change and Status Consumption. In A. S. Kotur & S. K. Dixit (Eds.), *The Emerald Handbook of Luxury Management for Hospitality and Tourism* (pp. 285–303). Emerald Publishing Limited.

Ante, L. (2021). The Non-Fungible Token (NFT) Market and its Relationship with Bitcoin and Ethereum. BRL Working Paper Series, No. 20.

Arcos, L. C. (2018). The Blockchain Technology on the Music Industry. *Brazilian Journal of Operations & Production Management, 15*(3), 439–443.

Atasoy, O., & Morewedge, C. K. (2018). Digital Goods Are Valued Less Than Physical Goods. *Journal of Consumer Research, 44*(6), 1343–1357.

Azzi, R., Chamoun, R. K., & Sokhn, M. (2019). The Power of a Blockchain-Based Supply Chain. *Computers & Industrial Engineering, 135*(1), 582–592.

Bal, F., & Nijkamp, P. (2001). In Search of Valid Results in a Complex Economic Environment: The Potential of Meta-analysis and Value Transfer. *European Journal of Operational Research, 128*(2), 364–384.

Balaji, M. S., & Roy, S. K. (2017). Value Co-Creation with Internet of Things Technology in the Retail Industry. *Journal of Marketing Management, 33*(1-2), 7–31.

Bamakan, S. M. H., Nezhadsistani, N., Bodaghi, O., & Qu, Q. (2022). Patents and Intellectual Property Assets as Non-Fungible Tokens: Key Technologies and Challenges. *Scientific Reports, 12*(1), 1–13.

Barakat, S., Yaghi, K., & Al-Zagheer, H. (2022). The Use of NFT for Patent Protection. *Advances in Dynamical Systems and Applications, 17*(1), 107–113.

Bartmanski, D., & Woodward, I. (2018). Vinyl Record: A Cultural Icon. *Consumption Markets & Culture, 21*(2), 171–177.

Bataille, P., & Perrenoud, M. (2021). "One for the Money"? The Impact of the "Disk Crisis" on "Ordinary Musicians" Income: The Case of French Speaking Switzerland. *Poetics, 86*, 1–13.

BBC. (2021). Side-Eyeing Chloe' Clem to Sell Iconic Meme as NFT. Retrieved March 12, 2022, from https://www.bbc.com/news/world-us-canada-58659667

Belk, R. W. (1984). Three Scales to Measure Constructs Related to Materialism: Reliability, Validity, and Relationships to Measures of Happiness. *Advances in Consumer Research, 11*(1), 291–297.

Belk, R. W. (1985). Materialism: Trait Aspects of Living in the Material World. *Journal of Consumer Research, 12*(3), 265–280.

Belk, R. W. (1988). Possessions and the Extended Self. *Journal of Consumer Research, 15*(2), 139–168.

Belk, R. W. (2013). Extended Self in a Digital World. *Journal of Consumer Research, 40*(3), 477–500.

Bell, G., & Gemmell, J. (2009). The E-Memory Revolution. *Library Journal, 134*(15), 20–23.

Benjamin, W. (1936/1969). The Work of Art in the Age of Mechanical Reproduction. In H. Arendt (Ed.), *Illuminations* (pp. 214–218). Schocken Books.

Berger, J., & Ward, M. (2010). Subtle Signals of Inconspicuous Consumption. *Journal of Consumer Research, 37*(4), 555–569.

Bolton, S. J., & Cora, J. R. (2021). Virtual Equivalents of Real Objects (VEROs): A Type of Non-Fungible Token (NFT) that Can Help Fund the 3D Digitization of Natural History Collections. *Megataxa, 6*(2), 93–95.

Bourgeon-Renault, D. (2000). Evaluating Consumer Behaviour in the Field of Arts and Culture Marketing. *International Journal of Arts Management, 3*(1), 4–18.

Braglia, M., Marrazzini, L., Padellini, L., & Rinaldi, R. (2020). Managerial and Industry 4.0 Solutions for Fashion Supply Chains. Journal of Fashion Marketing and Management: An. *International Journal, 25*(1), 184–201.

Bruner, G. C. (2013). *Marketing Scales Handbook: Multi-Item Measures for Consumer Insight Research* (Vol. 7). GCBII Productions.

Brynjolfsson, E., & Mcafee, A. (2017). Artificial Intelligence, for Real. *Harvard Business Review, 1*, 1–31.

Bsteh, S., & Vermeylen, F. (2021). From Painting to Pixel: Understanding NFT Artworks. Retrieved December 18, 2022, from http://www.researchgate.net/publication/351346278_From_Painting_to_Pixel_Understanding_NFT_artworks

Business of Fashion. (2021). The State of Fashion 2021 Report: Finding Promise in Perilous Times. Retrieved January 8, 2022, from https://www.businessof-fashion.com/reports/news-analysis/the-state-of-fashion-2021-industry-report-bof-mckinsey/

Chang, L., & Arkin, R. M. (2002). Materialism as an Attempt to Cope with Uncertainty. *Psychology & Marketing, 19*(5), 389–406.

Chaudhari, A. A., Laddha, D., & Potdar, M. (2019). Decentraland: A Blockchain-Based Model for Smart Property Experience. *International Engineering Journal for Research & Development, 4*(5), 5–15.

Chevet, S. (2018). Blockchain Technology and Non-Fungible Tokens: Reshaping Value Chains in Creative Industries. Retrieved December 12, 2021, from https://papers.ssrn.com/sol3/papers.cfm?abstract_id=3212662

Chohan, R., & Paschen, J. (2021, in press). *What Marketers Need to Know about Non-Fungible Tokens (NFTs)*. Business Horizons.

Ciaian, P., Rajcaniova, M., & Kancs, D. (2016). The Economics of BitCoin Price Formation. *Applied Economics, 48*(19), 1799–1815.

Cleveland, M., & Chang, W. (2009). Migration and Materialism: The Roles of Ethnic Identity, Religiosity, and Generation. *Journal of Business Research, 62*(10), 963–971.

Colbert, F. (2003). Entrepreneurship and Leadership in Marketing the Arts. *International Journal of Arts Management, 6*(1), 30–39.

Coleman, J. (2011). QR Codes: What Are They and Why Should You Care? *Kansas Library Association College and University Libraries Section Proceedings, 1*, 16–23.

Coletto, M., Aiello, L. M., Lucchese, C., & Silvestri, F. (2017). Adult Content Consumption in Online Social Networks. *Social Network Analysis and Mining, 7*(1), 1–21.

De Mauro, A., Greco, M., & Grimaldi, M. (2019). Understanding Big Data Through a Systematic Literature Review: The ITMI Model. *International Journal of Information Technology & Decision Making, 18*(04), 1433–1461.

Deloitte. (2022). From Trading Cards to Digital Video: Sports NFTs Kick Sports Memorabilia into the Digital Age. Retrieved March 5, 2022, from https://www2.deloitte.com/xe/en/insights/industry/technology/technology-media-and-telecom-predictions/2022/sports-nfts-digital-media.html

Demirbag, M., Sahadev, S., & Mellahi, K. (2010). Country Image and Consumer Preference for Emerging Economy Products: The Moderating Role of Consumer Materialism. *International Marketing Review, 27*(2), 141–163.

Denegri-Knott, J., & Molesworth, M. (2013). Redistributed Consumer Desire in Digital Virtual Worlds of Consumption. *Journal of Marketing Management, 29*(13-14), 1561–1579.

Dodds, W. B., Monroe, K. B., & Grewal, D. (1991). Effects of Price, Brand, and Store Information on Buyers' Product Evaluations. *Journal of Marketing Research, 28*(3), 307–319.

DressX. (2021). DressX Official. Retrieved January 15, 2022, from https://dressx.com

Dujak, D., & Sajter, D. (2019). Blockchain Applications in Supply Chain. In A. Kawa & A. Maryniak (Eds.), *SMART Supply Network* (pp. 21–46). Springer International Publishing.

Durham, J. (1965). Confusion of Fungible and Non-Fungible Goods. *Baylor Literature Review, 17*, 80–89.

Dwyer, G. P. (2015). The Economics of Bitcoin and Similar Private Digital Currencies. *Journal of Financial Stability, 17*(2015), 81–91.

Eastman, J. K., Fredenberger, B., Campbell, D., & Calvert, S. (1997). The Relationship Between Status Consumption and Materialism: A Cross-Cultural

Comparison of Chinese, Mexican, and American Students. *Journal of Marketing Theory and Practice*, 5(1), 52–66.

Eastman, J. K., Goldsmith, R. E., & Flynn, L. R. (1999). Status Consumption in Consumer Behavior: Scale Development and Validation. *Journal of Marketing Theory and Practice*, 7(3), 41–52.

Eladhari, M. (2007). The Player's Journey. In J. P. Williams & J. H. Smith (Eds.), *The Players' Realm: Studies on the Culture of Video Games and Gaming* (pp. 171–187). Jefferson, NC.

Erevelles, S., Fukawa, N., & Swayne, L. (2016). Big Data Consumer Analytics and the Transformation of Marketing. *Journal of Business Research*, 69(2), 897–904.

Evans, T. M. (2019). Cryptokitties, Cryptography, and Copyright. *AIPLA QJ*, 47, 219.

Fairchild. (2006). Fun and Easy Project. Retrieved November 12, 2021, from https://acnpsearch.unibo.it/journal/2255104

Focus. (2021). The First NFT Millionaire Made It Possible for Anyone to Earn $171,000 A Month by Investing. Retrieved January 18, 2022, from https://focus.com.au/first-nft-project-on-opensea

Forbes. (2021). NFTs, Metaverse and GameFi Are Changing Up the Fashion Business in 2022. Retrieved February 2, 2022, from https://www.forbes.com/sites/josephdeacetis/2021/12/22/nfts-metaverse-and-gamefi-are-changing-up-the-fashion-business-in-2022

Forbes. (2022). Why Video Game Makers See Huge Potential in Blockchain – And Why Problems Loom for Their New NFTs. Retrieved March 14, 2022, from https://www.forbes.com/sites/justinbirnbaum/2022/01/06/why-video-game-makers-see-huge-potential-in-blockchain-and-why-problems-loom-for-their-new-nfts/?sh=7be09e3b43d7

Fouce-Rodríguez, H. (2010). Technologies and Media in Digital Music: From Music Market Crisis to New Listening Practices. *Revista Comunicar*, 17(34), 65–71.

Fritze, M. P., Eisingerich, A. B., & Benkenstein, M. (2019). Digital Transformation and Possession Attachment: Examining the Endowment Effect for Consumers' Relationships with Hedonic and Utilitarian Digital Service Technologies. *Electronic Commerce Research*, 19(2), 311–337.

Fuentes, C., Hagberg, J., & Kjellberg, H. (2019). Soundtracking: Music Listening Practices in the Digital Age. *European Journal of Marketing*, 53(3), 483–503.

Gabler, J., Kropp, F., Silvera, D. H., & Lavack, A. M. (2004). The Role of Attitudes and Self-Efficacy in Predicting Condom Use and Purchase Intentions. *Health Marketing Quarterly*, 21(3), 63–78.

Gehl, R. W. (2021). Dark Web Advertising: The Dark Magic System on Tor Hidden Service Search Engines. *Continuum*, 35(5), 1–12.

Ger, G. (2005). Special Session Summary Religion and Consumption: The Profane Sacred. *Advances in Consumer Research*, 32(1), 79–81.

Ger, G., & Belk, R. W. (1996). Cross-cultural Differences in Materialism. *Journal of Economic Psychology, 17*(1), 55–77.

Girvan, C. (2018). What Is a Virtual World? Definition and Classification. *Educational Technology Research and Development, 66*(5), 1087–1100.

Goanta, C. (2020). Selling LAND in Decentraland: The Regime of Non-Fungible Tokens on the Ethereum Blockchain under the Digital Content Directive. In A. Lehavi & R. Levine-Schnur (Eds.), *Disruptive Technology, Legal Innovation, and the Future of Real Estate* (pp. 139–154). Springer International Publishing.

Goldsmith, R. E., & Clark, R. A. (2012). Materialism, Status Consumption, and Consumer Independence. *The Journal of Social Psychology, 152*(1), 43–60.

Goldsmith, R. E., Flynn, L. R., & Kim, D. (2010). Status Consumption and Price Sensitivity. *Journal of Marketing Theory and Practice, 18*(4), 323–338.

Goldsmith, R. E., Moore, M. A., & Beaudoin, P. (1999). Fashion Innovativeness and Self-Concept: A Replication. *Journal of Product & Brand Management, 8*(1), 7–18.

Gorkhali, A., Li, L., & Shrestha, A. (2020). Blockchain: A Literature Review. *Journal of Management Analytics, 7*(3), 321–343.

Grewal, D., Noble, S. M., Roggeveen, A. L., & Nordfalt, J. (2020). The Future of In-store Technology. *Journal of the Academy of Marketing Science, 48*(1), 96–113.

Grewal, D., Roggeveen, A. L., & Nordfält, J. (2017). The Future of Retailing. *Journal of Retailing, 93*(1), 1–6.

Guido, G. (2001). *The Salience of Marketing Stimuli: An Incongruity-Salience Hypothesis on Consumer Awareness.* Kluwer Academic Publishers.

Guido, G. (2002). Dalla Personalizzazione alla Virtualizzazione del Marketing dei Luoghi. In L. Biggiero & A. Sammarra (Eds.), *Apprendimento, Identità e Marketing del Territorio* (pp. 96–107). Carocci Editore.

Guido, G. (2014). *Il Comportamento di Consumo degli Anziani: Effetti per le Strategie di Marketing delle Imprese.* Il Mulino.

Guido, G., Amatulli, C., Peluso, A. M., De Matteis, C., Piper, L., & Pino, G. (2020). Measuring Internalized versus Externalized Luxury Consumption Motivations and Consumers' Segmentation. *Italian Journal of Marketing, 4*(1), 1–23.

Guido, G., Prete, M. I., Pichierri, M., Pino, G., & Peluso, A. M. (2016). *Beyond Ethical Consumption: Religious-like Behaviours and Marketing Habits for Fervid Attachment to Brands.* Peter Lang.

Gupta, S. S. (2017). Blockchain: IBM Online. Retrieved December 23, 2021, from http://www.ibm.com

Hair, J. F., Black, W. C., Babin, B. J., & Anderson, R. E. (2013). *Multivariate Data Analysis.* Pearson.

Hayes, A. F. (2022). *Introduction to Mediation, Moderation, and Conditional Process Analysis: A Regression-Based Approach.* The Guilford Press.

Hirsch, F. (1976). *Social Limits to Growth*. Harvard University Press.

Hirunyawipada, T., & Paswan, A. K. (2006). Consumer Innovativeness and Perceived Risk: Implications for High Technology Product Adoption. *Journal of Consumer Marketing*, *23*(4), 182–198.

Hoffman, D. L., Kopalle, P. K., & Novak, T. P. (2010). The "Right" Consumers for Better Concepts: Identifying Consumers High in Emergent Nature to Develop New Product Concepts. *Journal of Marketing Research*, *47*(5), 854–865.

Hogg, N., & Jackson, T. (2009). Digital Media and Dematerialization: An Exploration of the Potential for Reduced Material Intensity in Music Delivery. *Journal of Industrial Ecology*, *13*(1), 127–146.

Hoyer, W. D., Kroschke, M., Schmitt, B., Kraume, K., & Shankar, V. (2020). Transforming the Customer Experience through New Technologies. *Journal of Interactive Marketing*, *51*(1), 57–71.

Immink, K. A. (1998). The Compact Disc Story. *Journal of the Audio Engineering Society*, *46*(5), 458–465.

Johnson, J. A. (2010). To Catch a Curious Clicker: A Social Network Analysis of the Online Pornography Industry. In K. Boyle (Ed.), *Everyday Pornography* (pp. 22–43). Routledge.

Jung, H., Bardzell, S., Blevis, E., Pierce, J., & Stolterman, E. (2011). How Deep Is Your Love: Deep Narratives of Ensoulment and Heirloom Status. *International Journal of Design*, *5*(1), 59–71.

Kietzmann, J., Lee, L. W., McCarthy, I. P., & Kietzmann, T. C. (2020). Deepfakes: Trick Or Treat? *Business Horizons*, *63*(2), 135–146.

Kim, H. Y., Lee, J. Y., Mun, J. M., & Johnson, K. K. (2017). Consumer Adoption of Smart In-Store Technology: Assessing the Predictive Value of Attitude Versus Beliefs in the Technology Acceptance Model. *International Journal of Fashion Design, Technology and Education*, *10*(1), 26–36.

Kim, J. (2021). Advertising in the Metaverse: Research Agenda. *Journal of Interactive Advertising*, *21*(3), 141–144.

Kleine, S. S., & Baker, S. M. (2004). An Integrative Review of Material Possession Attachment. *Academy of Marketing Science Review*, *1*(1), 1–39.

Kosík, M. (2011). Marketing Strategy in Connection with Sport. *Marketing*, *7*(2), 92–98.

Krohn-Grimberghe, L. (2020). The Dematerialization of Music: How Streaming Technology Impacts Music Production and Consumption. In M. Trondle (Ed.), *Classical Concert Studies* (pp. 296–308). Routledge.

Kwong, S. W., & Park, J. (2008). Digital Music Services: Consumer Intention and Adoption. *The Service Industries Journal*, *28*(10), 1463–1481.

Laskowski-Jones, L. (2020). Living and Dying in a Virtual World. *Nursing*, *50*(7), 6–15.

Lawry, C. A., & Choi, L. (2013). The Omnichannel Luxury Retail Experience: Building Mobile Trust and Technology Acceptance of Quick Response (QR) Codes. *Marketing ZFP, 35*(2), 144–154.

Lee, E. (2021). The Bored Ape Business Model: Decentralized Collaboration via Blockchain and NFTs. Retrieved November 30, 2021, from https://doi.org/10.2139/ssrn.3963881

Lee, E. (2022). NFTs as Decentralized Intellectual Property, SSRN. Retrieved December 14, 2022, from https://papers.ssrn.com/sol3/papers.cfm?abstract_id=4023736

Londono, J. C., Davies, K., & Elms, J. (2017). Extending the Theory of Planned Behavior to Examine the Role of Anticipated Negative Emotions on Channel Intention: The Case of an Embarrassing Product. *Journal of Retailing and Consumer Services, 36,* 8–20.

Louis Vuitton. (2022). Louis Vuitton Collection for League of Legends. Retrieved March 6, 2022, from https://it.louisvuitton.com/ita-it/magazine/articoli/league-of-legends-collection

Lynch, S., & Barnes, L. (2020). Omnichannel Fashion Retailing: Examining the Customer Decision-Making Journey. *Journal of Fashion Marketing and Management: An International Journal, 24*(3), 471–493.

Magaudda, P. (2011). When Materiality 'Bites Back': Digital Music Consumption Practices in the Age of Dematerialization. *Journal of Consumer Culture, 11*(1), 15–36.

Masataka, N. (2007). Music, Evolution and Language. *Developmental Science, 10*(1), 35–39.

Maxmudjanovna, A. I., Abdurasulovna, P. R., & Erkinovna, N. N. (2020). The Future of the Digital Economy: Concept and Role of Blockchain Technologies. *Journal of Critical Reviews, 7*(8), 1812–1818.

Mortensen, T. E. (2007). Mutual Fantasy Online: Playing with People. In J. P. Williams & J. H. Smith (Eds.), *The Players' Realm: Studies on the Culture of Video Games and Gaming* (pp. 188–211). Jefferson, NC.

Musictech. (2021). Artists Are Selling Their Music as NFTs – And They're Making Millions. Retrieved December 21, 2021, from https://www.musictech.net/news/artists-selling-music-nft-making-millions/

Nadini, M., Alessandretti, L., Di Giacinto, F., Martino, M., Aiello, L. M., & Baronchelli, A. (2021). Mapping the NFT Revolution: Market Trends, Trade Networks, and Visual Features. *Scientific Reports, 11*(1), 1–11.

Nguyen, B., & Simkin, L. (2017). The Internet of Things (IoT) and Marketing: The State of Play, Future Trends and the Implications for Marketing. *Journal of Marketing Management, 33*(1-2), 1–6.

Nofer, M., Gomber, P., Hinz, O., & Schiereck, D. (2017). Blockchain. Business & Information. *Systems Engineering, 59*(3), 183–187.

Nssmag. (2021). A Study of Fashion Brand Perception 2021. Retrieved January 12, 2022, from https://data.nssmag.com/docs/CARTESIO

O'Cass, A., & Frost, H. (2002). Status Brands: Examining the Effects of Non-Product-Related Brand Associations on Status and Conspicuous Consumption. *Journal of Product & Brand Management, 11*(2), 67–88.

O'Cass, A., & McEwen, H. (2004). Exploring Consumer Status and Conspicuous Consumption. *Journal of Consumer Behaviour, 4*(1), 25–39.

O'Dwyer, R. (2020). Limited Edition: Producing Artificial Scarcity for Digital Art on the Blockchain and Its Implications for the Cultural Industries. *Convergence, 26*(4), 874–894.

Odom, W., Zimmerman, J., & Forlizzi, J. (2010). Virtual Possessions. In: Proceedings of the 8th ACM Conference on Designing Interactive Systems, Aarhus, Denmark, August 16-2, 368–371.

Odom, W., Zimmerman, J., & Forlizzi, J. (2011). Teenagers and Their Virtual Possessions: Design Opportunities and Issues. In *Proceedings of the International Conference on Human Factors in Computing Systems*, Vancouver, Canada, May 7–12, pp. 1491–1500.

Ogden, J. R., Ogden, D. T., & Long, K. (2011). Music Marketing: A History and Landscape. *Journal of Retailing and Consumer Services, 18*(2), 120–125.

Okonkwo, U. (2009). Sustaining the Luxury Brand on the Internet. *Journal of Brand Management, 16*(5), 302–310.

Oliveira, L., Zavolokina, L., Bauer, I., & Schwabe, G. (2018). To Token Or Not to Token: Tools for Understanding Blockchain Tokens. Retrieved December 28, 2021, from https://www.zora.uzh.ch/id/eprint/157908/

OpenSea. (2021). OpenSea: Browse NFT. Retrieved March 8, 2022, from https://opensea.io/assets

Panciroli, C., Russo, V., & Macauda, A. (2017). When Technology Meets Art: Museum Paths Between Real and Virtual. *Multidisciplinary Digital Publishing Institute Proceedings, 9*(1), 913–927.

Panda, S., & Palejwala, D. A. (2020). Effectiveness of Meme Marketing. Retrieved December 13, 2021, from https://repository.iimb.ac.in/handle/2074/19460

Pantano, E., & Dennis, C. (2019). Store Buildings as Tourist Attractions: Mining Retail Meaning of Store Building Pictures Through a Machine Learning Approach. *Journal of Retailing and Consumer Services, 51*, 304–310.

Park, J. E., Yu, J., & Zhou, J. X. (2010). Consumer Innovativeness and Shopping Styles. *Journal of Consumer Marketing, 27*(5), 437–446.

Park, J. S., Ha, S., & Jeong, S. W. (2020). Consumer Acceptance of Self-Service Technologies in Fashion Retail Stores. *Journal of Fashion Marketing and Management: An International Journal, 25*(2), 372–388.

Park, S., Specter, M., Narula, N., & Rivest, R. L. (2021). Going from Bad to Worse: From Internet Voting to Blockchain Voting. *Journal of Cybersecurity, 7*(1), 25–31.

Patrickson, B. (2021). What do Blockchain Technologies Imply for Digital Creative Industries? *Creativity and Innovation Management, 30*(3), 585–595.

Peluso, A. M., Pino, G., Amatulli, C., & Guido, G. (2017). Luxury Advertising and Recognizable Artworks: New Insights on the "Art Infusion" Effect. *European Journal of Marketing, 51*(11/12), 2192–2206.

Pilkington, M. (2016). Blockchain Technology: Principles and Applications. In F. X. Olleros & M. Zhegu (Eds.), *Research Handbook on Digital Transformations* (pp. 41–48). Edward Elgar Publishing.

Rae, M. (2021). Analyzing the NFT Mania: Is a JPG Worth Millions? In *SAGE Business Cases.* SAGE Publications, Ltd. Retrieved July 17, 2021, from https://doi.org/10.4135/9781529779332

Raman, R., & Benson, E. R. (2021). The World of NFTs (Non-Fungible Tokens): The Future of Blockchain and Asset Ownership. In B. M. Adel & L. Chaari Fourati (Eds.), *Enabling Blockchain Technology for Secure Networking and Communications* (pp. 89–108). IGI Global.

Richins, M. L. (1994). Special Possessions and the Expression of Material Values. *Journal of Consumer Research, 21*(3), 522–533.

Richins, M. L. (2004). The Material Values Scale: Measurement Properties and Development of a Short Form. *Journal of Consumer Research, 31*(1), 209–219.

Richins, M. L., & Dawson, S. (1992). A Consumer Values Orientation for Materialism and Its Measurement: Scale Development and Validation. *Journal of Consumer Research, 19*(3), 303–316.

Rodeschini, S. (2021). New Standards of Respectability in Contemporary Pornography: Pornhub's Corporate Communication. *Porn Studies, 8*(1), 76–91.

Rogers, S. (2020). PornVisory Lays Out Its Blockchain Future. Retrieved December 22, 2021, from https://gritdaily.com/pornvisory-blockchain-future/

Rolling Stone. (2021). Rolling Stone and Coinbase Are Collaborating with 12 Artists on an Exclusive NFT Drop. Retrieved November 28, 2021, from https://www.rollingstone.com/culture/culture-features/rolling-stone-and-coinbase-nft-drop-1292861/

Saberi, S., Kouhizadeh, M., Sarkis, J., & Shen, L. (2019). Blockchain Technology and Its Relationships to Sustainable Supply Chain Management. *International Journal of Production Research, 57*(7), 2117–2135.

Schaar, L., & Kampakis, S. (2022). Non-Fungible Tokens as an Alternative Investment: Evidence from CryptoPunks. *The Journal of the British Blockchain Association, 5*(1), 31949–31959.

Scitovsky, T. (1976). *The Joyless Economy: An Inquiry into Human Satisfaction and Consumer Dissatisfaction.* Oxford University Press.

Seok, B., Park, J., & Park, J. H. (2019). A Lightweight Hash-Based Blockchain Architecture for Industrial IoT. *Applied Sciences, 9*(18), 3740–3745.

Serada, A., Sihvonen, T., & Harviainen, J. T. (2021). CryptoKitties and the New Ludic Economy: How Blockchain Introduces Value, Ownership, and Scarcity in Digital Gaming. *Games and Culture, 16*(4), 457–480.

Sestino, A., Amatulli, C., & De Angelis, M. (2021a, in press). Retail e Nuove Tecnologie nel Fashion: Effetti su Shopping Experience e Brand "Luxuryfication". Micro & Macro Marketing.

Sestino, A., Amatulli, C., & Guido, C. (2021b). The Effect of Consumers' Innovativeness and Conspicuous Consumption on Environmentalism. A Study in the Context of Smart Mobility. *Technology Analysis & Strategic Management*, *1*, 1–14.

Sestino, A., & De Mauro, A. (2021). Leveraging Artificial Intelligence in Business: Implications, Applications and Methods. *Technology Analysis & Strategic Management*, *34*(1), 16–29.

Sestino, A., Giraldi, L., Cedrola, E., & Guido, G. (2022). The Relevance of Individuals' Perceived Data Protection Level on Intention to Use Blockchain-Based Mobile Apps. An Experimental Study. In M. Al-Emran (Ed.), *Recent Innovations in Artificial Intelligence and Smart Applications*. Springer International Publishing, in press.

Sestino, A., Prete, M. I., Piper, L., & Guido, G. (2020). Internet of Things and Big Data as Enablers for Business Digitalization Strategies. *Technovation*, *98*(C), 102173–102181.

Sestino, A., Prete, M. I., Piper, L., & Guido, G. (2021). The Future of Online Marketing Strategies and Digital Tools: New Challenges and Contribution to the RACE Framework. *International Journal of Electronic Trade*. https://doi.org/10.1504/IJETRADE.2021.10042594

Shah, D., Patel, D., Adesara, J., Hingu, P., & Shah, M. (2021). Exploiting the Capabilities of Blockchain and Machine Learning in Education. *Augmented Human Research*, *6*(1), 1–14.

Sharma, H. (2018). Memes in Digital Culture and Their Role in Marketing and Communication: A Study in India. *Interactions: Studies in Communication & Culture*, *9*(3), 303–318.

Shifman, L. (2013). Memes in a Digital World: Reconciling with a Conceptual Troublemaker. *Journal of Computer-Mediated Communication*, *18*(3), 362–377.

Siddiqui, N., O'Malley, A., McColl, J. C., & Birtwistle, G. (2003). Retailer and Consumer Perceptions of Online Fashion Retailers: Web Site Design Issues. *Journal of Fashion Marketing and Management: An International Journal*, *7*(4), 345–355.

Singh, J., & Singh, P. (2021). Distributed Ownership Model for Non-Fungible Tokens. *Smart and Sustainable Intelligent Systems*, *12*, 307–321.

Singhal, B., Dhameja, G., & Panda, P. S. (2018). How Blockchain Works. In B. Singhal, G. Dhameja, & P. S. Panda (Eds.), *Beginning Blockchain* (pp. 31–148). Apress.

Sinn, D., Kim, S., & Syn, S. Y. (2017). Personal Digital Archiving: Influencing Factors and Challenges to Practices. *Library Hi Tech*, *35*(2), 222–239.

Song, J. Y., Chang, W., & Song, J. W. (2019). Cluster Analysis on the Structure of the Cryptocurrency Market via Bitcoin-Ethereum Filtering. *Physica A: Statistical Mechanics and Its Applications, 527*, 121339–121345.

Sportico. (2021). NFT Boom Leaves a Crypto or Cash Conundrum for Teams and Athlete. Retrieved March 8, 2022, from https://www.sportico.com/business/finance/2021/sports-nft-sales-crypto-1234629061/

Stafford, S. A. (2010). Music in the Digital Age: The Emergence of Digital Music and Its Repercussions on the Music Industry. *The Elon Journal of Undergraduate Research in Communications, 1*(2), 112–120.

Steenkamp, J. B. E., & Gielens, K. (2003). Consumer and Market Drivers of the Trial Probability of New Consumer Packaged Goods. *Journal of Consumer Research, 30*(3), 368–384.

Stephenson, N. (2003). *Snow Crash: A Novel.* Spectra.

Stewart, D. W., & Zhao, Q. (2000). Internet Marketing, Business Models, and Public Policy. *Journal of Public Policy & Marketing, 19*(2), 287–296.

Sylim, P., Liu, F., Marcelo, A., & Fontelo, P. (2018). Blockchain Technology for Detecting Falsified and Substandard Drugs in Distribution: Pharmaceutical Supply Chain Intervention. *JMIR Research Protocols, 7*(9), e10163–e10172.

The Guardian. (2021). A Virtual Steal: The Digital Gucci Sneakers for Sale at $17.99. Retrieved November 11, 2021, from https://www.theguardian.com/fashion/2021/mar/19/a-virtual-steal-the-gucci-sneakers-for-sale-at-1799

Themistocleous, M. (2018). Blockchain Technology and Land Registry. *Cyprus Review, 30*(2), 195–202.

Tripathi, G., Tripathi Nautiyal, V., Ahad, M. A., & Feroz, N. (2021). Blockchain Technology and Fashion Industry-Opportunities and Challenges. *Blockchain Technology: Applications and Challenges, 12*(19), 201–220.

Veer, E., & Shankar, A. (2011). Forgive Me, Father, for I Did Not Give Full Justification for My Sins: How Religious Consumers Justify the Acquisition of Material Wealth. *Journal of Marketing Management, 27*(5-6), 547–560.

Venkatesh, A., & Meamber, L. A. (2006). Arts and Aesthetics: Marketing and Cultural Production. *Marketing Theory, 6*(1), 11–39.

Vigneron, F., & Johnson, L. W. (1999). A Review and a Conceptual Framework of Prestige-Seeking Consumer Behavior. *Academy of Marketing Science Review, 1*(1), 1–15.

Vigneron, F., & Johnson, L. W. (2004). Measuring Perceptions of Brand Luxury. *Journal of Brand Management, 11*(6), 484–506.

Vogue. (2021). Dolce & Gabbana Porta gli NFT nel Mondo della Moda. Retrieved December 30, 2022, from https://www.vogue.it/moda/article/dolce-gabbana-ntf-haute-couture-moda-venezia

Vogue Business. (2021). The 'Baby Birkin' NFT and the Legal Scrutiny on Digital Fashion. Retrieved January 30, 2022, from https://www.voguebusiness.com/technology/the-baby-birkin-nft-and-the-legal-scrutiny-on-digital-fashion

Vujičić, D., Jagodić, D., & Ranđić, S. (2018). Blockchain Technology, Bitcoin, and Ethereum: A Brief Overview. In *17th International Symposium INFOTEH-JAHORINA (INFOTEH)*, pp. 1–6.

Waldfogel, J. (2017). How Digitization Has Created a Golden Age of Music, Movies, Books, and Television. *Journal of Economic Perspectives, 31*(3), 195–214.

Wanberg, C. R., & Banas, J. T. (2000). Predictors and Outcomes of Openness to Changes in a Reorganizing Workplace. *Journal of Applied Psychology, 85*(1), 132.

Wang, Q., Li, R., Wang, Q., & Chen, S. (2021). Non-Fungible Token (NFT): Overview, Evaluation, Opportunities and Challenges. Retrieved December 1, 2021, from https://arxiv.org/abs/2105.07447

Watkins, R. D., Denegri-Knott, J., & Molesworth, M. (2016). The Relationship Between Ownership and Possession: Observations from the Context of Digital Virtual Goods. *Journal of Marketing Management, 32*(1-2), 44–70.

Whitaker, A., Bracegirdle, A., de Menil, S., Gitlitz, M. A., & Saltos, L. (2021). Art, Antiquities, and Blockchain: New Approaches to the Restitution of Cultural Heritage. *International Journal of Cultural Policy, 27*(3), 312–329.

Wilson, K. B., Karg, A., & Ghaderi, H. (2021, in press). Prospecting Non-Fungible Tokens in the Digital Economy: Stakeholders and Ecosystem, Risk and Opportunity. Business Horizons. https://doi.org/10.1016/j.bushor.2021.10.007.

Wired. (2021). NFT e Musica. Perché Sono Fatti l'Uno per l'Altro? Retrieved October 31, 2021, from https://www.wired.it/play/musica/2021/07/03/nft-musica-funzionano/

Wong, N. Y. (1997). Suppose You Own the World and No One Knows? Conspicuous Consumption, Materialism and Self. *Advances in Consumer Research, 24*, 197–203.

Workman, J. E., & Johnson, K. K. (1993). Fashion Opinion Leadership, Fashion Innovativeness, and Need for Variety. *Clothing and Textiles Research Journal, 11*(3), 60–64.

Wu, T. Y., Tseng, Y. M., Huang, S. S., & Lai, Y. C. (2017). Non-Repudiable Provable Data Possession Scheme with Designated Verifier in Cloud Storage Systems. *IEEE Access, 5*, 19333–19341.

Wu, Y., & Ardley, B. (2007). Brand Strategy and Brand Evolution: Welcome to the World of the Meme. *The Marketing Review, 7*(3), 301–310.

Yee, N., & Bailenson, J. (2007). The Proteus Effect: The effect of Transformed Self-representation on Behavior. *Human Communication Research,* *33*(3), 271–290.

Zhai, S., Yang, Y., Li, J., Qiu, C., & Zhao, J. (2019). Research on the Application of Cryptography on the Blockchain. *Journal of Physics: Conference Series,* *1168*(3), 032077–032089.

Zhang, T., & Huang, X. (2021). Viral Marketing: Influencer Marketing Pivots in Tourism: A Case Study of Meme Influencer Instigated Travel Interest Surge. *Current Issues in Tourism, 10,* 1–8.

Zhou, H. (2018). Characteristics of User Experience in Art E-commerce: Case "Buybuy Art". Retrieved November 28, 2021, from https://trepo.tuni.fi/handle/10024/103861

INDEX

© The Author(s), under exclusive license to Springer Nature   97
Switzerland AG 2022
A. Sestino et al., *Non-Fungible Tokens (NFTs)*,
https://doi.org/10.1007/978-3-031-07203-1

The manufacturer's authorised representative in the EU is Springer
Nature Customer Service Centre GmbH, Europaplatz 3, 69115 Heidelberg,
Germany. If you have any concerns regarding our products, please
contact ProductSafety@springernature.com

Printed and bound by CPI Group (UK) Ltd, Croydon, CR0 4YY

29/04/2026

02099478-0015